HOME WITH HONOR

HOME
WITH
HONOR

HELPS FOR RETURNING MISSIONARIES

RANDY L. BOTT

Deseret Book Company
Salt Lake City, Utah

Library of Congress Cataloging-in-Publication Data

Bott, Randy L., 1945–
    Serve with honor : helps for returning missionaries / Randy L. Bott.
        p.   cm.
    Includes bibliographical references and index.
    ISBN 0-87579-956-6 (pbk.)
    1. Church of Jesus Christ of Latter-day Saints—Missions.
2. Missionaries, Resignation of. 3. Missionaries—Religious life.
4. Spiritual life—Church of Jesus Christ of Latter-day Saints.
I. Title.
BX8661.B679   1995
266'.9332—dc20
                                       95-33309
                                         CIP

Printed in the United States of America
10 9 8 7 6 5 4 3 2   49510-4713B

To those faithful missionaries
who have discovered that coming home
can be as demanding as adjusting to the mission field—
but who refuse to lose that cutting edge
they developed on their missions

CONTENTS

CONTENTS

RETURN WITH HONOR

CONGRATULATIONS! You have just completed the most difficult task that God requires of his faithful sons and daughters to this point in their lives. If you served with honor, you probably had mixed feelings about coming home. You wanted to stay and continue in the work that has become a way of life for you, but you were also ready to move on to an exciting future. Unfortunately, you can't do both!

You were called for eighteen months or for two years of missionary service, and now it is time to turn your attention to the future. You may feel as if you are breaking a rule as you spend so much time considering your options. The objective of this book is to give you some ideas about things you may want to consider. Ideas for this book came over a three-year period while I served as a mission president with my wife. Many returned missionaries told us that coming home is a more difficult adjustment than entering the mission area. These young men and women didn't want to lose the spiritual growth they had achieved, and they wanted to know how to live so they wouldn't "fall off the table" spiritually as they entered into the uncharted territory of social life, marriage, career, and raising a family. It is hoped that the practical advice given here will lessen the difficulty of your reentry into civilian life.

This book focuses on practical, reasonable ideas that are

gospel-related. This book is not intended to be an exhaustive scriptural treatise. The scriptures themselves should be your handbook for successful living. Although various scriptures will be cited, the major emphasis of the book will be on the principles behind the scriptures. Inspiring quotes from various Church leaders will be used.

A lifetime study of the scriptures and the latter-day prophets will "lead the man [or woman] of Christ in a strait and narrow course across that everlasting gulf of misery which is prepared to engulf the wicked—and land their souls, yea, their immortal souls, at the right hand of God in the kingdom of heaven, to sit down with Abraham, and Isaac, and with Jacob, and with all our holy fathers, to go no more out" (Helaman 3:29–30).

This book is a compilation of ideas and thoughts we found helpful as we counseled missionaries who were about to return home. However, it is not intended to replace the advice you receive from your local priesthood leaders. I have tried to avoid "fringe doctrine" or advice that would lead you away from the kingdom of God. My hope is that this book will help you make good decisions, establish good habits, and rededicate yourself or continue to dedicate yourself to living the gospel, that you may find real joy in life. The final portion of the book will present practical advice aimed at helping you find an eternal companion.

The challenge in life is to find a Christlike balance. Before your mission you may have emphasized sports or dating or academic development far more than you emphasized spiritual development. During your mission, your main focus was on spiritual development. Yes, your intellectual understanding of the gospel also grew at an awe-inspiring rate, but that was not your main objective. Now that you are returning home, you may wonder if your spiritual development over-shadows the other three areas. Or you may discover that instead of being overdeveloped spiritually, you have just now caught up in that crucial area.

If all of these four aspects of your life—spiritual, intellectual, social, and physical—are in proper balance, your life will proceed more smoothly. If any one of the four areas gets too much emphasis or is neglected, the results will be evident as you lose your balance and become a little lopsided. If the imbalance continues, the very foundations of your spiritual well-being may be shaken. Although there may be times when one area is emphasized, that is not normal or desirable as a permanent state. During the next few years, for example, you may focus on completing school. If you postpone your spiritual development until your schooling is complete, however, you may not be motivated to return to developing this important aspect of your life later on.

Serious evaluation and proper perspective will help you avoid getting out of balance. Members do not lose their testimonies or fall away from the Church unless they neglect opportunities to consult with God and to get his divine input on how to solve problems. Prayer and scripture study are so important that they need to be mentioned even in this introductory chapter.

The other factor that will help you maintain a proper balance is your willingness to study and follow the counsel of the living prophets. You will never fall away into forbidden paths if you heed the counsel of those whom God has chosen to guide us through these difficult times.

Again, congratulations on completing a successful mission. Now let's talk about moving forward in the great game of life.

2

BEING RELEASED WITHOUT RETURNING

ALMOST ALL MISSIONARIES I have worked with and interviewed are afraid of coming home and losing their spirituality. You have worked hard to make progress. You may have seen other returned missionaries literally *return* to their old ways, tossing to the wind their spirituality, testimony, and Christlike lifestyle. Yet I have never talked to a missionary yet who planned on reverting back to old ways when he or she was released. What can you do to ensure that this does not happen to you?

It begins with getting rid of the term *returned* and replacing it with *released*. Forget the idea of going back. Even if you want to, you will never be able to fit back into life exactly the way you did before you left. Most friends will have changed. Some will be married, others will still be serving missions, some will be away at school, and others will have full-time jobs. A few will be about the same as when you left. You will probably wonder how they could be so concerned with things you now think are of absolutely no consequence. Some will still live to party every night. They look forward not to the second coming of Christ but to the concert next month or the dance this weekend. They rarely, if ever, consider their eternal future or welfare. You will probably not be as inclined to be close friends with them as you thought you would be. Your value systems are too different. Your interests are too diverse. These old buddies may want to include you in their circle of friends, but you will soon discover that the condition they attach is that you join them in their parties and activities. When you attend their parties but refuse to drink or participate in unwholesome things, it will make them uncomfortable. They know they are doing wrong, and your continued presence will only put a damper on their "fun." Don't be surprised if you are invited less and less often to join them.

How do you keep from feeling a spiritual drop when your stake president releases you? You probably will feel a drop, but it doesn't have to be a dramatic drop—just a dip. If you feel the need, ask the stake president to give you a blessing when he releases you. His inspired counsel may give you direction that will make your readjustment easier. Your father or another Melchizedek Priesthood holder could also give you a blessing. The Lord is not going to abandon you because you have completed your mission. However, you will probably come to a sober realization of how much your Heavenly Father was sustaining you (or even carrying you!) during your mission.

Full-time missionaries are not the only ones who are entitled to have the Spirit as a constant companion. If you stay active in missionary-related activities and other righteous pursuits, the Spirit will stay with you.

If you show the least bit of interest in missionary work when you return, you may be called to a position involving missionary work in your new ward or stake. When I was a recently released missionary from Samoa, I was called to be a stake missionary. At the request of a neighbor friend, I taught

his aunt the six discussions. It was a fiasco! I had to say everything in Samoan and then translate it into English. If the
gospel were not true and the Spirit were not willing to make
up for my inadequacies, she never would have joined. But
she did join! The next week the stake president called me to
be the first counselor in the stake mission presidency. Before
very many months, the stake mission president was called to
be a bishop, and at the ripe old age of twenty-one I was
called as the new stake mission president—an office that I
held and loved until I was married at age twenty-four. I
believe that it was the stake mission experience that helped
me learn how to teach the gospel in English.

If you are not called on a stake mission, that certainly
does not mean that you can't do missionary work. Remember how disappointed you were when members weren't very
involved in missionary work? Well, now you are one of those
members! Let's see how you perform. You may live in an area
where there are very few who are not members of the
Church. Don't let that stop you. Many people need to have
their testimonies revived from smoking embers into flaming
fires. You can do that even without a formal calling. How?
Think back to what you did to bring the Spirit into a missionary discussion. You prayed, read scriptures, shared spiritual experiences, sang songs, resolved concerns, and so on.
Those same principles will revive the spiritually sleeping.
What a wonderful resource you are for the bishop; you can
help him perfect the Saints. In losing yourself in the service
of others, you will find yourself (see Matthew 16:25).

Released missionaries who spend their time pushing
people from the ends of the earth towards Zion (see D&C
58:45) will not fall. It is only when you focus on yourself that

you begin to shrivel spiritually. Service cures the spiritual doldrums!

Another way to continue growing spiritually is to intensify your study of the scriptures. Many returned missionaries are still trying to teach the "specialty lessons" they developed in the mission field. As great as those lessons may have been, you need to keep growing. Without some added effort, the crispness of gospel knowledge and scriptural insight will grow stale with the passing of time.

You may have known the most scriptures in the entire mission, but compared to what there is to know about the scriptures, there is still much to learn. Some returned missionaries give the impression that they know "all that God has revealed, all that He does now reveal" (Article of Faith 9), and many things that He has not revealed. In a priesthood or Sunday School class, these returned missionaries just sit pompously back and sneer at the struggling teacher when a class discussion is floundering.

Other returned missionaries humbly recognize that they know relatively little compared to how much there is to know. They are like sponges: they soak up knowledge, understanding, and insight. They ask questions for their own understanding but also to help clarify principles that they know but that others are struggling to grasp. When they attend a Sunday School or other auxiliary class, they take some of the responsibility for how the class is going. If the discussion is dragging, they try to help the teacher be successful.

Regular, ongoing scripture study is a part of your continuing spiritual growth and development. Chapter four, "Sensible Scheduling," discusses how to establish a realistic study schedule. If you feel the Spirit decreasing, evaluate your scripture study.

An important way to ensure that the Spirit does not withdraw is to pray. Remember in the mission field when an investigator was not progressing as planned? Very often when you asked these individuals about their follow-through on the scripture reading and prayer commitments, they would answer, "No, I'm just not comfortable praying!" When investigators would pray, read the scriptures, and attend church, they were almost assured of gaining the desired testimony unless other parts of their lives were grossly out of focus.

So it is with you. If you become lax in your prayers, either in frequency or sincerity, the Spirit withdraws. Remember Nephi's wise counsel: "It grieveth me that I must speak concerning this thing. For if ye would hearken unto the Spirit which teacheth a man to pray ye would know that ye must pray; for the evil spirit teacheth not a man to pray, but teacheth him that he must not pray" (2 Nephi 32:8). Mormon emphasized sincerity, saying, "And likewise also it is counted evil unto a man, if he shall pray and not with real intent of heart; yea, and it profiteth him nothing, for God receiveth none such" (Moroni 7:9).

There is nothing magical about the formula for getting the Spirit while on your mission, and there isn't anything magical about keeping it when you return home. Service, scripture study, and prayer work every time. Consciously striving to live righteously will not be difficult if you decide that you will not allow a day to pass without using all three of these keys. If you do that, you will never lose your spirituality.

READJUSTING TO YOUR FAMILY

ONE OF THE MOST FRIGHTENING prospects for a missionary preparing to return home is facing the issue of fitting into the family again. To those who have never served a mission, that may seem like a trivial issue. But the issue is real.

First, you have changed a lot in the last year and a half or two years. The advantage is that no one at home knows what you are like now! You may find that there are still a few things that need correcting or adjusting in your personality. If minor changes can be made by simply making a conscious decision, make the changes before you go home. You can decide to keep your room cleaner, to help out more around the house, or to consciously make an effort to be more complimentary to those around you. But be realistic. If your mission has helped you identify some major character flaws or areas of difficulty in your interpersonal relationships, working on these challenges will probably require more time, effort, and practice than you have available before ending your mission. You don't need to worry; people will be surprised and pleased with the changes and progress you have made.

Second, don't try to put on a facade. Be yourself. No one appreciates insincerity. Once you've been released by the stake president, you will no longer be a full-time, ordained minister. Your role is not to call your family to repentance. As you learned on your mission, stewardship goes from the top down, not from the bottom up! When you return home, remind yourself, if necessary, that your parents lead the family, not you. Whether your father is a General Authority or a nonmember, you will probably find things you think ought to be changed. Resist the urge to repair all the wrongs in the family.

A friend told me about his call to be a General Authority. He felt out of place being around brethren who were spiritual and wise. He consulted with his sheepherder father about what to say and how to act. This wise father gave some very timely advice: "Oh, son," he said, "just graze around the edges for a while." In other words, watch how things operate. Be more visible than vocal. There will be plenty of time and opportunities to make helpful suggestions.

Third, be an example of what you believe rather than a voice in the wilderness. You will probably be told often to "give yourself a few weeks and you'll get your feet on the ground. You'll get back to normal soon enough." Unfortunately, many missionaries fulfill that prophecy. Your loved ones will watch you carefully for signs that indicate you are getting back to the old you. If you stay with your resolve to "never go back" to those habits and personality traits you have resolved to eliminate from your life, others may still expect you to fall off your ivory tower of righteousness sooner or later.

When days become weeks and weeks evolve into months and the expected change does not take place, you will begin to enjoy the fruits of your righteous example. As Nicodemus came to Christ at night and alone, so members of your family and others may come to you away from the spotlight.

They will want to know why you continue to be happy. Why doesn't anything get you down? When they ask those questions, you can invite them to a higher level of understanding. One startling occurrence is that other returned missionaries may come to you for advice.

Often the person who wants your advice will be the person who seems to be totally happy in their life of sin. The one no one would expect is struggling to change. When friends or family members of this kind admit they're really miserable, you'll probably be very surprised.

After years of watching closely those who have chosen to disobey God's laws, I have an abiding testimony that Alma was right: "Wickedness never was happiness" (Alma 41:10). Many people want to be happy, but, like the Nephites, they "have sought all the days of [their] lives for that which [they] could not obtain; and [they] have sought for happiness in doing iniquity, which thing is contrary to the nature of that righteousness which is in our great and Eternal Head" (Helaman 13:38).

When others seek your counsel, do what you did in the mission field—teach them a better way. Don't preach, condemn, ridicule, or mock, but be kind, gentle, and understanding. If you do not set a proper example, you will not have the desired impact.

Fourth, avoid the desire to be everything to everybody. You may find that you have more time on your hands than you had on your mission (unless you get into school immediately). At first you may feel restless. You may feel that you are wasting valuable time or that nothing you do is as satisfying as missionary work. Those feelings are normal and expected. Because you have become accustomed to making every minute count, your initial reaction when you return home is to fill every free moment with activity. Soon you will be faced with a different frustration—you won't have enough time to do everything. It is best to slowly ease into a full schedule. Demands will change as time passes.

At first Mom and Dad may want to show you off to relatives and friends. You will no doubt be asked to speak in sacrament meeting, and in addition you may serve as a speaking companion to a high council member when he addresses a ward on his assigned Sunday. You may be asked to speak at your mom's club party, at firesides, or at youth conferences. You may be asked to give the lesson at enlarged family home evenings or even give a portion of Mom's Relief Society lesson. These activities generally subside after a few months.

The more definite your postmission plans, the easier it is to adopt a reasonable schedule. It will be long-range commitments that become burdensome as your normal schedule fills.

Fifth, act—don't react. In an attempt to help you "get real," your little brother or sister may say or do things to irritate you or to provoke a fight. If you have already thought through these potentially explosive situations, you will have some idea of how to defuse the confrontation. Humor is a great relaxer. So are cheerfulness and optimism. Decide beforehand to respond cheerfully and, if possible, humorously to family conflicts.

What will you do if your family decides on a family picnic that interferes with your church meetings? What if your mom asks you to make a purchase at the store on Sunday? You may never have to face these situations, but you can probably anticipate several potentially uncomfortable situations you may face with family members. Decide before you leave the mission area how to handle them so you don't appear self-righteous or make your family feel like vile sinners.

Sixth, watch for the teaching moments. There will be moments when it becomes apparent that "now is the right time." If you live each day with a prayer in your heart, asking Heavenly Father to keep you ready to be his voice, you will be surprised how often opportunities come. Examples from your mission teach powerful lessons. I would emphasize again, avoid the temptation to preach!

Seventh, if you fail to progress because your parents are trying to re-exert excessive control, be wise enough to leave home. As long as you live with them, expect to be governed by their rules.

As your light continues to shine within the walls of your own home, it will illuminate even the darkest corners. Other family members will grow because of your example. But don't expect too much too fast. Change happens slowly. One of the promised rewards for being an honorably returned missionary is that your family will be blessed.

4

....

Avoiding Spiritual Elitism

For the past eighteen months or two years you have focused on spiritual things. If you have served with honor, you are probably at your highest level spiritually ever. Spiritual maturity is just the beginning of the blessings and rewards that your Heavenly Father has promised you. When Heavenly Father blesses us with any quality of character, the adversary tries to get us to use it to our destruction. Spiritual growth is no exception.

Because the adversary has enjoyed nearly six thousand years of experience with the many billions of our brothers and sisters, he has become an expert in deception. Unfortunately, some people have not exercised sufficient staying power to resist his temptations. Satan may use individuals who have distanced themselves from the mainstream of the Church for his evil purposes. Many of these people honestly believe that they are spiritually superior. They steadfastly maintain their allegiance to the Church and its leaders, but they claim that because of their spiritual superiority, they are able to live laws higher than those presently being taught by the prophets. How convenient!

You may be approached by someone who seems to be very spiritual who says something like, "I perceive by the Spirit that you are a cut above others in your family or in your ward. I am therefore authorized to invite you to join a select group." Neither out of curiosity or vanity should you ever accept such an invitation. Whenever anyone tells me that my spirituality exempts me from living certain commandments and authorizes me to live a "higher" set of commandments, that is an immediate red flag. If the Savior did not excuse himself from even the least commandment, why should some people think they—or anyone else—should have special spiritual privileges? Avoid these people. When you say, "No, I must live by the same rules that everyone else lives by," they may very well respond by saying, "Perhaps I have misinterpreted what the Spirit is saying. I guess you are not really among the spiritually elite!" Bid them a good day, and get on with your life.

If you have been diligent in studying the gospel and applying it in the mission field, you will have made great spiritual strides, and you may receive many compliments. Recognize growth, but use it to bless others, not to pat yourself on the back. The only one from whom we really want to hear, "Well done, thou good and faithful servant" is the Lord. He does that by leaving his Spirit with us.

Satan may try to make you believe that you really are smarter because you know many scriptures. He may try to get you to think you are more spiritual than others because you seem to be doing more of what Heavenly Father has asked us to do. Remember the Lord's stern warning in Doctrine and Covenants 82:3: "For of him unto whom much is given much is required; and he who sins against the greater light shall receive the greater condemnation." It may even be true that you are more familiar with the scriptures and the teachings of latter-day prophets than anyone in the ward. They may not have enjoyed the uninterrupted months of gospel focus that you have. Stay humble by reminding your-self that unless you continue to study and seek the guidance of the Spirit, you may find that when you have been home from your mission as long as they have, your spiritual knowl-edge may diminish too.

One of the real problems faced by returning missionar-ies is avoiding the label "gospel know-it-all" that comes nat-urally when you respond to every question in the Sunday School class. How can you be true to your testimony and knowledge and avoid the label? It isn't easy! What generally happens is that you answer a question posed by the teacher that no one else seems to know how to answer. Your answer is scripturally based or documented by a quote from a latter-day prophet. Everyone in class is impressed with your wis-dom. The teacher may even be a bit intimidated. The next question is asked directly to you because the teacher and class members love the spirit that comes when you answer the Lord's way. You answer. The pattern is set. The class is in danger of becoming a dialogue between you and the teacher.

How do you avoid or break that cycle? In class itself you might try buying a little time. A question is posed to you. You know the answer but are uncomfortable answering every question. You might say something like, "That is a really good question. I'd like to hear what some of the others in class have to say about that." You might also respond by saying, "I'll need a minute to think about that question. What do others have to say?" A sensitive teacher will understand what you are doing and willingly solicit input from other class members.

If that doesn't work, you can meet the teacher before or after class and explain that you feel uncomfortable answer-ing more than your share of questions in class. You might even suggest that you'd be glad to discuss gospel principles with him or her any time, but Sunday School really needs to be a learning experience for everyone. Almost always the teacher will find ways to broaden classroom discussions and help others feel their contributions are worthwhile. In the rare instance when everything else fails, attend the Gospel Essentials class instead of Gospel Doctrine.

More frequently the problem will be one of false doctrine being taught by a teacher who isn't quite as well-versed as you would hope. As you discovered in the mission field, there are two distinct and separate gospels. One is the revealed gospel, and the second is the "hearsay gospel." The hearsay gospel is the easiest to master because you don't have to document anything. You merely have to say, "I heard that . . . !" When you hear doctrine taught that is questionable or clearly false, you are seldom in a position to stand up and, with the pointing finger of scorn, rebuke the person teaching the false doctrine. That would show extremely poor taste anyway. There are ways of helping teachers of "hearsay doctrine" realize that false doctrine will not be tolerated.

First, you might say, "That is really interesting doctrine. Could you give me a reference or a place where I might study more about it?" That will generally bring the "hearsay" response, "Well, I'm not sure where that is found, but I'm sure I heard it somewhere!" You can then calmly suggest that the class adopt the ground rule to accept only doctrine from the scriptures and the latter-day prophets. A second method might be to say, "I am having difficulty reconciling that teaching with these scriptures that seem to teach the opposite. Could you help me understand?" It doesn't take very long until the "hearsay gospel" scholar chooses to keep his opinions to himself because the embarrassment of being challenged by the scriptures or prophets is too great.

If the false doctrines continue, you might ask the bishop how to handle it. He may be aware of the problem and even be working behind the scenes to eliminate the source. A word of caution—don't try to right every wrong. There will be slips of the tongue or slightly misstated issues that are not technically correct but are not potentially fatal. If you choose to challenge every little error (as you may suppose), you will quickly be labeled as a troublemaker instead of being a strength to the class or quorum. Choose carefully your battlefields. Most people recognize when the teacher or person commenting in class is off-base.

Be extremely careful not to "magnify" the bishop's office. You may feel that you could organize the ward, call people to offices, counsel those in trouble, or move the ward spiritually forward better than the bishop. There's only one problem: that is his office and calling and not yours! If you want to feel the Spirit withdraw in a hurry, just get out ahead of the bishop. Whether he is right or wrong, good or bad, he is the Lord's anointed and the Lord will bless his decisions. Give help where you can, preferably when you are asked. Avoid criticizing the bishop or other ward leaders in your conversations. Remember in the mission field how frustrated it made you feel when ward members would criticize you behind your back? If you want to help a person perfect himself or herself and grow, go directly to that person.

Someday you may be called as the bishop or Relief Society president. Then you will discover that the calling isn't as easy as it looks! Right now, do everything in your power to help others succeed in their callings. Make them look good. Don't worry about whether you get credit for what you do. You will be blessed for it. Magnify your own calling and be of service to others when you can.

Remembering that the Lord knows the end from the beginning, you can rest assured that you need not waste your time "campaigning for position." Many truly great leaders in the Church will tell you the same thing: just grow wherever you are planted. If the Lord wants you in a position, he will maneuver you until you are there. Experience has proven that those who campaign the hardest for Church positions are often the least qualified to hold the office. At times it has been amusing and disappointing to see how many people openly campaign to become a mission president. Although serving as mission president was a great honor, it isn't something a person would campaign to become. Those who are called humbly accept and do the best they know how. At the end of three years, I doubt that anybody requests an extension. So it is with callings of bishops, Relief Society presidents, stake presidents, and other positions of high profile—but also of extreme pressure and demand.

The Lord knows where he wants you to serve. If you are willing and pliable, he will give you experiences that will help you grow. We should not tell the Lord where we want to serve and for how long. Instead, we need to be humble and recognize that the Lord is still directing his work.

You can do much more good if you are not worried about who gets the credit. Until the Second Coming, when everyone will be rewarded according to their works, there will be those who are willing to stand up and take credit for work that others do—and they then have their reward. Go quietly about doing good wherever you can. If you are not recognized or even found out—so much the better. Start the "mystery love basket" in your ward—just a little basket to let somebody know that someone else cares. Include a little note suggesting that they anonymously pass the basket on. In wards where that practice has been started, it has brought joy and excitement where boredom and complacency have been. No one needs know who decided to prove again that it really is more blessed to give than to receive. What joy you will bring to your ward as you go about doing good without hoping for or expecting a reward.

5

....

SENSIBLE SCHEDULING

NOT LONG AFTER I STARTED teaching seminary, I had a group of rowdy senior students. During the course of the year, they matured a lot. I learned more about teaching and they learned more about the gospel. At the end of the year, only one young man was still a trial. He would sit on the back row and pull the hair of the girl who sat in front of him or put his feet over her shoulders. It became a challenge to get anyone to sit near him. Toward the end of the school year we took a class period and had everyone tell their plans for the future. To everyone's surprise this young man said he was preparing for a mission. Everyone laughed, but he steadfastly maintained he was going. A few months later I received a phone call from him. He wanted me to speak at his farewell, and of course I accepted.

Two years passed before I knew it. One day after school I was sitting in my office when in walked a clean-cut, mature young man with a large binder under one arm and a set of scriptures under the other. I thought it was another of the many salesmen who frequently came to sell their products.

The young man asked, "Brother Bott, don't you recognize me?" I studied his vaguely familiar face and had to admit that I couldn't place him. He introduced himself as the rowdy boy from my seminary class, and then he told me about his very successful mission. Then I started to probe. "How do you plan to keep the spirituality you developed in the mission field?" To which he responded, "I thought you might ask, so I brought my plan." He laid out the large binder containing many sections. He showed me how he had organized the gospel into subjects. As he read the scriptures or talks from the modern prophets, he entered the passage into one or more of the categories. By the time he had worked his way through the scriptures and the conference talks, he would have enough material to write a book about any topic in the gospel. I was impressed but leery. "When are you going to do all this?" I asked. He explained how he planned to get up every morning at 6:00 A.M., study for two hours, get ready for the day, and either go to school or work. I asked whether he thought he could keep the schedule; he assured me that he could. We parted after a few more minutes of small talk.

About three months later I was walking down the main street of Logan, Utah, when I heard a whistle and a call from the far side of the street: "Brother Bott!" From across the street I saw a grubby-looking, bearded guy head toward me. I thought for a minute that my number had just been called. This man grabbed me by the shoulders and gave me a big hug. I must have looked bewildered, because he stood back and said, "You don't recognize me, do you?" I admitted that I didn't. When he told me that he was the "Mr. Clean" who had reported from his mission three months earlier, I almost fell over!

I asked what had happened to him, and he replied that he had left my office, reported his mission that next Sunday, started his study schedule on Monday, and continued it on Tuesday and Wednesday. Then he realized that he had bitten off more than he could chew. He put his scriptures away, stopped attending Church, and reverted back to his old ways. He said it wasn't until he saw me that he realized how far he'd slipped in such a short time. I asked him why he didn't just decrease his study time. He said he didn't know why, but he hadn't. We talked for some time. He promised to get back into shape spiritually and to come see me often. He did both. Eventually he was sealed to a lovely young woman in the temple, and the last I heard, he was doing well.

This kind of thing happens over and over again. You need to face the fact that you will likely not be able to maintain the study schedule you established on your mission. Before you leave the mission field, you should set some realistic study goals. If you get home and discover that the press of life makes it impossible to keep up the planned study pace, cut back. If you can't study for an hour every day, try studying for a half hour. If you can't do that, resolve to read a chapter of scripture a day. If you can't do that, then read at least a few verses every day. You cannot expect to maintain your spiritual muscles if you don't feed them, any more than you would expect to sustain your physical muscles if you went on a starvation diet.

Set a specific time every day to study, preferably in the morning. If you start the day by learning the things of God, whenever you have a spare minute during the day, your mind will revert back to what you learned earlier. Note the Lord's counsel to "arise early, that your bodies and your *minds* may be invigorated" (D&C 88:124; emphasis added).

Establish a specific place to study. Avoid studying on the bed. You will find soon enough that life after a mission is often lived in the fast lane. If you lie down on your bed, you will probably fall asleep. Get a desk, sit at the kitchen table, find an overstuffed chair in the living room, or choose some other convenient place to study. Have your scriptures handy so you don't have to waste valuable study time hunting for them.

Determine a course of study. It might be the Sunday School Gospel Doctrine course for the year. Explore those topics that interest you. Stay with the mainstream of the doctrine. The standard works will never lead you astray. Read the talks and writings of the latter-day prophets. Select very carefully beyond that. Many books provide valuable insight; but in some books, the author tries to reveal things that the Lord, in his wisdom, has chosen to keep secret. Avoid speculative doctrine. It is one of Satan's tools to lure you into forbidden paths.

Because the gospel is both spiritual and practical, there is the temptation to try to experience the entire gospel all at once. However, your spiritual progress cannot be forced. It must be allowed to mature and unfold naturally. Running faster than you have the spiritual strength or foundation to sustain will result in the adversary taking advantage of you.

Many people humbly study the gospel for the personal insight that Heavenly Father promises to give the faithful. Others seem impatient with how long it takes to build a spiritual foundation. In an attempt to accelerate their learning, they meet together in study groups. That sounds innocent enough, but sad experience has proven that unless you are cautious and have some strict guidelines, you could find yourself focusing on a narrow part of the gospel or on a "fringe doctrine"—an intriguing but nonessential area of gospel study. Note carefully the promise and caution the Lord gives:

> For thus saith the Lord—I, the Lord, am merciful
> and gracious unto those who fear me, and delight to

honor those who serve me in righteousness and in truth unto the end.

Great shall be their reward and eternal shall be their glory.

And to them will I reveal all mysteries, yea, all the hidden mysteries of my kingdom from days of old, and for ages to come, will I make known unto them the good pleasure of my will concerning all things pertaining to my kingdom.

Yea, even the wonders of eternity shall they know, and things to come will I show them, even the things of many generations.

And their wisdom shall be great, and their understanding reach to heaven; and before them the wisdom of the wise shall perish, and the understanding of the prudent shall come to naught.

For by my Spirit will I enlighten them, and by my power will I make known unto them the secrets of my will—yea, even those things which eye has not seen, nor ear heard, nor yet entered into the heart of man. (D&C 76:5–10)

Elsewhere the Lord, through the prophet Alma, issues the caution, "It is given unto many to know the mysteries of God; nevertheless they are laid under a strict command that they shall not impart only according to the portion of his word which he doth grant unto the children of men, according to the heed and diligence which they give unto him" (Alma 12:9).

Elder Boyd K. Packer also gave the following timely counsel:

I have come to believe also that it is not wise to continually talk of unusual spiritual experiences. They are to be guarded with care and shared only when the Spirit itself prompts us to use them to the blessing of others. . . . A testimony is not thrust upon you; a testimony grows. . . . It is not wise to wrestle with the revelations with such insistence as to demand immediate answers or blessings to your liking. You cannot force spiritual things. . . . Do not be impatient to gain great spiritual knowledge. Let it grow, help it grow; but do not force it, or you will open the way to be misled. ("Candle of the Lord," address given to mission presidents June 25, 1982)

I have been invited many times to join study groups. I have declined because of the counsel of the Brethren and because my first priority is to teach and be an example to my family. By the time I finish that never-ending task, there isn't the time or the inclination to become involved beyond those organized study sessions the Lord has provided each of us during our Sunday meetings.

A wise man once said, "When we focus on a single doctrine of the gospel with the intent of learning all about it, we soon know more and more about less and less until we know everything about nothing!" The Lord needs you to be faithful and diligent in these last days. When you start to explore one single doctrine or a fringe doctrine, you may end up being unable to carry the burden of leadership to which you were foreordained.

Look at your mission president, stake president, or bishop. These men are not prone to delve constantly in the thick of thin things. They are mainstream people; follow their example. Pace yourself and make it your goal to gradually gain a deeper understanding of the gospel's essential, saving doctrines.

Gospel Scholarship
without Apostasy

When missionaries learn to "feast upon the words of Christ" (2 Nephi 32:3), they discover how sweet the word really is. There is a temptation to let personal study encroach on proselyting time. This urge is generally suppressed, because you know that there will be plenty of time when you return home to satisfy that hunger. Now you are home and find yourself back in the fast lane. Schooling often becomes an emerging priority as you try to find balance between social activities, work, school, and church. It is not unusual for a returned missionary to long for the good old days in the mission field when everything was so simple.

Many men and women have served missions; fewer have continued to actively study the gospel and scriptures with the same intensity they applied to the task while serving a mission. Unless you make a special effort, you may find yourself in the same category a few years from now. Many young men and women attend school for years after their missions and become experts in their chosen professions and yet believe that a few minutes every once in a while will result in their becoming gospel scholars! If you want to become a scholar, you must plan to devote countless hours to serious, concentrated study. Gospel scholarship itself is neither good nor bad. Whether that scholarship moves you closer to your Heavenly Father or pulls you further from him is the crucial factor. Jacob, who could perhaps be considered the "intellectual" of the Book of Mormon, said, "But to be learned is good *if* they hearken unto the counsels of God" (2 Nephi 9:29; emphasis added). However, a quick reading of the preceding verse enlarges Jacob's concern: "O that cunning plan of the evil one! O the vainness, and the frailties, and the foolishness of men! When they are learned *they think they are wise,* and they hearken not unto the counsel of God, for they set it aside, supposing they know of themselves, wherefore, their wisdom is foolishness and it profiteth them not. And they shall perish" (2 Nephi 9:28; emphasis added).

How do you develop into a gospel scholar? Daily study over an extended period of time is a more effective method than studying for large blocks of time every once in a while. When you systematically investigate the gospel and take particular note of how each doctrine and topic interrelates with all the others, you begin to gain insight never attained through casual reading. Time to ponder, meditate, compare, and contrast is necessary to deepen your understanding. Reading for speed does not bring deep insight.

When you study the scriptures, consider the meaning of each word. Then zoom out and look at the positioning of the verse. How does it fit within the chapter, the book, or the entire volume of scripture? Try to understand the principle behind the scripture. Perhaps the actual setting of the particular verse may be irrelevant, but the principle may be vital. For example, after Lehi recounted his inspired dream to Laman and Lemuel, Nephi records that "he did exhort them then with all the feeling of a tender parent, that they would hearken to his words, that perhaps the Lord would be merciful to them, and not cast them off; yea, my father did preach unto them. And after he had preached unto them, and also prophesied unto them of many things, he bade them to keep the commandments of the Lord; and he did cease speaking unto them" (1 Nephi 8:37–38). As interesting as the story is, and as much as we may empathize with Lehi, part of the real value comes as we consider how he (a struggling father) dealt with his wayward sons: he realized that there is a time to quit and let natural consequences teach the next level of lessons. Unless we can extract principles from the scriptures and apply those principles in our lives, they are interesting stories but little else. Serious gospel scholars who pay the price to find the hidden treasures in the scriptures are promised that they will "enjoy the words of eternal life in this world, and eternal life in the world to come, even immortal glory" (Moses 6:59).

Searching for lists, noting cause-and-effect passages, looking for divine definitions, understanding symbolism and veiled phrases, allowing the Lord to interpret his own scriptures, and using external sources for clarification provide rich and rewarding paybacks for your hours of intense scriptural study. Don't rush to know it all. Spiritual knowledge comes when you are prepared to receive it. Provide a fertile mind in which the thoughts can grow, then allow Heavenly Father to nurture them in "his own time, and in his own way, and according to his own will" (D&C 88:68).

Satan may try to take advantage of your enthusiasm for things of the Spirit. His counterfeit knowledge leads to personal apostasy. At this point in your life, you may be concerned about the risks associated with becoming a Mormon "intellectual." During a conversation with me, one bright

Latter-day Saint scholar noted, "Self-designated 'Mormon intellectuals' are neither. They disqualify themselves from being 'Mormons' because they no longer subscribe to the discipline and beliefs of the Mormons, and they certainly are not 'intellectuals' when they match their own weak mental processes against the infinite knowledge of God!"

One of the sure signs that the quest for intellectual understanding is leading a person astray is outlined by the Prophet Joseph Smith: "I will give you one of the Keys of the mysteries of the Kingdom. It is an eternal principle, that has existed with God from all eternity: That man who rises up to condemn others, finding fault with the Church, saying that they are out of the way, while he himself is righteous, then know assuredly, that that man is in the high road to apostasy; and if does not repent, will apostatize, as God lives" (*Teachings of the Prophet Joseph Smith,* sel. Joseph Fielding Smith [Salt Lake City: Deseret Book Company, 1938], 156–57).

As you increase in scholarship, follow closely the teachings of the Brethren and the scriptures. I have found it helpful to use the standard works as a guide. If the standard works say very little or nothing about a doctrine, maybe I should follow suit. Too many self-designated intellectuals choose to endlessly discuss those matters about which God has chosen to say little or nothing. Follow the living prophets. If they are not speaking about certain topics, follow their example. The Lord's law of safety for the scholar is found in Doctrine and Covenants 52:9: "And let them journey from thence preaching the word by the way, *saying none other things than that which the prophets and apostles have written,* and that which is taught them by the Comforter through the prayer of faith" (emphasis added).

If you should start to question the inspired leadership of those the Lord has raised up to lead his people during these crucial days, you'd be wise to stand back and look at the fate of those who have chosen to let go of the iron rod. Satan plays on the vanity of self-styled intellectuals. After all, they should be "bright enough" to think for themselves. I may not presently have sufficient information to understand the whys behind all the counsel the leaders are giving, but I do have a testimony that the Lord will never allow his chosen leaders to lead the Saints astray. Safety lies in following the guidelines that come from our leaders in Salt Lake City.

As you grow in your understanding of the gospel, remain teachable. If the only people you will learn from are those with higher academic degrees, more publications, or a higher Church position than you have, you will miss out on learning many of the most profound lessons of life. Remember the promise of the Lord through the Prophet Joseph Smith: "And not only this, but those things which never have been revealed from the foundation of the world, but have been kept hid from the wise and prudent, shall be revealed unto babes and sucklings in this, the dispensation of the fulness of times" (D&C 128:18). What a shame if we ever get too big in our own eyes to learn from little children.

The stronger your understanding becomes, the more powerful your voice will be in defending the kingdom of God. Many times you may wish that you had known a certain doctrine or scripture while you were on your mission. As your ability to defend your beliefs becomes more solid, you may have many opportunities to reason with others whose intellectual pursuits have weakened their faith. God is not anti-intellectual—provided we don't become puffed up to the point of "outgrowing" God. Frequently check your allegiance to God, the Church, and the Brethren and make whatever corrections are necessary.

What a thrill to listen to a person with a testimony who has really studied the gospel. I am fortunate to work with many men and women who are true "spiritual intellectuals" and whose testimonies are firm and unshakable. Does the Church discourage us from thinking for ourselves? Absolutely not. Just the opposite is true. The Lord has wisely provided guidelines to protect us from being led astray by Satan, "a liar from the beginning" (D&C 93:25). Even the highway department provides lines to keep us from straying off into dangerous and forbidden paths, where a costly crash is imminent and a fatal wreck is probable. Would the Almighty choose to do less?

7

No Mediocrity in Spirituality

You may look back on your mission and think that the trials and temptations you experienced during that time will never have an equal. If you believe that, you are in for a shock. Life is meant to be a test to prepare you to eventually become like your Heavenly Father. The Lord explained through Brigham Young, "My people must be tried in all things, that they may be prepared to receive the glory that I have for them, even the glory of Zion; and he that will not bear chastisement is not worthy of my kingdom" (D&C 136:31). The testing period has only begun.

It is fortunate that the tests will not come all at once. The Lord comforted us by saying, "For he will give unto the faithful line upon line, precept upon precept; and I will try you and prove you herewith" (D&C 98:12). Each time we prove our faithfulness and obedience, the Lord gives us additional light. He then showers us with more blessings, which bring additional revelations, which reveal even more commandments—and the cycle continues. The cycle is outlined in Doctrine and Covenants 59:4: "And they shall also be crowned with blessings from above, yea, and with commandments not a few, and with revelations in their time—they that are faithful and diligent before me."

You may not always see the wisdom behind the trial. In Doctrine and Covenants 58:3 the Lord cautions, "Ye cannot behold with your natural eyes, for the present time, the design of your God concerning those things which shall come hereafter, and the glory which shall follow after much tribulation." Our attitude in life is the crucial factor. To believe that God is punishing you or to accuse him of not making good on his promises of peace and prosperity in return for your missionary service would demonstrate a lack of understanding. Trials and tests come to everyone, even—or perhaps especially—to those who will be sanctified and prepared for the celestial kingdom (see D&C 101:4–5).

Many Latter-day Saints need your vision to help put their trials in proper perspective. If you whine and complain about trials, you not only postpone passage of the test but you destroy the confidence of those who are not well schooled spiritually and look to you for an example. Remember from your mission experience that the Spirit withdraws not only when you sin but also when you are ready to be tested or taught on a higher level.

When you notice a decrease in the intensity of the Spirit, ask whether you are breaking any additional commandments that you were not breaking earlier, when you strongly felt the guidance of the Spirit. If you are not, consider thanking your Heavenly Father for the confidence he is showing in allowing you to take a higher test on the trail toward perfection. Identify the test, and through faithful, humble diligence, pass it, thus qualifying yourself to take an even more difficult test. Is there an end? What is in it for you if you complete all the tests successfully? Joseph Smith gave an enlightening answer:

After a person has faith in Christ, repents of his sins, and is baptized for the remission of his sins and receives the Holy Ghost, (by the laying on of hands), which is the first Comforter, then let him continue to humble himself before God, hungering and thirsting after righteousness, and living by every word of God, and the Lord will soon say unto him, Son, thou shalt be exalted. When the Lord has *thoroughly proved him, and finds that the man is determined to serve Him at all hazards,* then the man will find his calling and his election made sure. (*Teachings of the Prophet Joseph Smith,* 150; emphasis added)

Certain goals you can set will challenge you to the limit. You have probably climbed higher up the mountain of spirituality than you ever dreamed you would; however, you are not yet standing atop the mountain. For eighteen months or two years you have been giving. To sustain your spiritual progress, you must learn to give for the rest of your life. When returned missionaries fall into a spiritual slump, their spiritual superiority becomes mediocrity when they just do nothing!

The people in the Church are moving onward and upward. If your graph line is flat, then what is righteousness to you today becomes wickedness tomorrow unless you improve on it. There is no stagnation in the kingdom of God. That seems to be where some returned missionaries make their mistake. They want to coast for a while. But you can only coast downhill! If you have tried to push-start a stalled car, you know how much easier it is to keep the car rolling than it is to stop and start pushing again. The same principle holds true in spiritual things. Now that you have spiritual momentum, keep rolling. Keep learning, growing, progressing, and climbing, and you won't be in danger of apostasy.

The first six months after your release seem to be the most critical. If you can get your feet on the ground after you get home, establish an acceptable routine, keep active in the Church, and maintain your spirituality, there isn't a great likelihood that you will become inactive. Before I returned home from my mission in Samoa, I wrote myself a letter. I first congratulated myself on successfully completing the mission, then started asking myself questions. It was like a PPI (personal priesthood interview), with me interviewing myself. "How are you doing in your daily prayers? Are you reading from the scriptures every day? Are you keeping your mind clear of polluting thoughts? Is your relationship with young ladies clean and wholesome?" The questions went on and on. I signed my name, put the letter in an envelope, postdated it for six months later, and sealed it up.

After being home two or three months, I found the letter and, eager to see what I had written, opened it. It was a real attention getter. I wasn't doing anything terribly wrong, but I just wasn't being as diligent in a few areas as I had promised I would be. There wasn't anyone to get angry at; after all, it was me telling myself to shape up. The final statement of my letter really hit home: "Now, Elder Bott, if you have slipped in any of the above areas, shape up! Your eternal life depends on it!" I had signed it, "With your eternal interest in mind, your brother, Elder Bott." I remember sitting in my bedroom and making some serious recommitments. For the next two or three months, I reread the letter once a week. My course was set, and that has carried me through the trials of the next quarter of a century. I am so thankful for that letter.

Maybe you should, while you still enjoy the spirit of the mission, write yourself a letter. If you're just not the writing type, at least hold a personal priesthood interview with yourself every Sunday before taking the sacrament. If you will do that for three or four months, you will find yourself stabilized and less likely to stray onto forbidden paths. Then once a month for the rest of your life (possibly on fast Sunday), hold the same kind of worthiness interview.

It isn't until you check your trajectory and speed that you become aware (if you are straying) that you could miss the celestial target altogether! Frequent midcourse corrections are easy to make. It is when we ignore the warnings and insist on traveling along forbidden paths that the corrections we must make to restore ourselves are major and painful. Frequent, small corrections are much more effective in helping us keep the Spirit than infrequent, massive alterations.

You may know a better method of making it through the adjustment period. If so, use it—but remember, you need a game plan. Most returned missionaries comment that it is more difficult to readjust to normal living than it was to adjust to being on a mission. If you are fully aware that your reentry into civilian life will not be without challenges, you will not be as likely to be taken by surprise by the adversary.

Talking about your mission helps crystalize the lessons you learned. As you discuss your mission with those who are planning on serving a mission in the future, be honest. You don't have to dredge up every bad thing that happened to you on your mission. However, you are not doing a very good job of informing the prospective missionary about real missionary life if you sugarcoat your experience. Too many missionaries arrive in the mission field believing that just showing up is all that is necessary to be a successful missionary. You can help them by truthfully discussing your mission.

Although difficult, your mission was definitely worth the sacrifice many times over. I have heard it said that a well-served mission is equivalent to fifty years of normal Church service. With a fifty-year head start, you should be able to move confidently into the next important chapter of life. The lessons you have learned, the principles you have mastered, the spiritual skills you have developed, your thirst for righteousness, and your determination to earn exaltation will never leave you if you don't leave them. You have agreed to follow God in the course that leads to eternal life. Remember his timely counsel: "For God doth not walk in crooked paths, neither doth he turn to the right hand nor to the left, neither doth he vary from that which he hath said, therefore his paths are straight, and his course is one eternal round" (D&C 3:2). If you don't leave the "strait and narrow path," you never need worry about losing your spirituality.

Lean on the Lord for help, and trust his unfailing promise: "Be of good cheer, for I will lead you along. The kingdom is yours and the blessings thereof are yours, and the riches of eternity are yours. And he who receiveth all things with thankfulness shall be made glorious; and the things of this earth shall be added unto him, even an hundred fold, yea, more" (D&C 78:18–19).

PHYSICAL APPEARANCE

SERVING A MISSION MAY have required a change in your dress habits. If you were prone to push the acceptable limits with hair length or clothing style before your mission, you may be tempted to return to the old ways. Before doing so, consider a statement by President Spencer W. Kimball:

> I want you to know it is hard for me to be disappointed, and I rejoice in the blessings of the Lord daily. But a few things disappoint me occasionally and one of them is the returned missionary who, after two years of taking great pride in how he looks and what he represents, returns to [a college] campus or some other place to see how quickly he can let his hair grow, how fully he can develop a moustache and long sideburns and push to the very margins of appropriate grooming, how clumpy his shoes [can] get, how tattered his clothes, . . . how close to being grubby he can get. . . . That, my young returned missionary brethren, is one of the great disappointments in my life. . . .
>
> Please, you returned missionaries and all young men who can understand my concern in this matter, please do not abandon in appearance or principle or habit the great experiences of the mission field when you were

like Alma and the sons of Mosiah, as the very angels of God to the people you met and taught and baptized. We do not expect you to wear a tie, white shirt, and a dark blue suit every day now that you are back in school. But surely it is not too much to ask that your good grooming be maintained, that your personal habits reflect cleanliness and dignity and pride in the principles of the gospel you taught. We ask you for the good of the kingdom and all those who have done and yet do take pride in you. (*The Teachings of Spencer W. Kimball* [Salt Lake City: Bookcraft, 1982], 593)

We enthusiastically sing, "We thank thee, O God, for a prophet"—why? "To guide us in these latter days"! It may seem a small matter to you, but you have joined a select group of chosen sons and daughters of God who were willing to sacrifice everything and respond to a call from a living prophet. You will always represent the effects, both positive and negative, that a mission has on people.

You might be tempted to respond, "Well, if others get offended at the way I dress, that is their problem!" Not so. Since you have promised in holy places to sacrifice and consecrate your all to the Lord for the furtherance of his kingdom, you must seriously consider the impact your dress and behavior has on everyone you meet. If you draw attention to yourself and away from the cause you represent, you are inappropriately dressed.

It is difficult to believe that young men and young women would be willing to give up virtually everything in their lives to proclaim the gospel only to return home and undermine all they have worked for by their sloppy appearance. Look at it this way: some day you'll be a parent of teenagers, and, believe me, you'll be struggling to encourage them to follow reasonable dress standards. Your parents—their grandparents—will get out the old photo albums, and there you'll be. How do you want to look in those photos? Like a young rebel, or like a person who knows where he or she is going in life?

Wearing shorts of the proper length seems to be a real challenge for returning missionaries. It may be true that your garments ride up on your legs to the point that some shorts could be worn. That old teenage attitude of "what can I get away with" should have been conquered in the mission field. The truly Christlike attitude is "What is the intent of the law?" The intent is that the garments should cover the knee. As you return to the temple often and participate in the ordinances, you will be reminded of the real purpose of the garment. Those who have matured spiritually see how subtle the adversary is and how he can lead you into forbidden paths. It is vital to take advantage of every help that Heavenly Father has given us to overcome Satan. One of those steps is wearing the temple garment properly.

Other than the instructions God gave to Adam and Eve before expelling them from the Garden of Eden, the only other thing he did was clothe them. The fad and fashion of the day is to suntan as much of the body as possible, almost without regard to modesty. To subject yourself to Satan by removing your temple garments for practically every common outdoor activity would not be demonstrating much understanding of how Satan operates and how much destructive power he has. Nor would that kind of behavior show how committed you are to continuing to keep your temple covenants.

The way we dress reflects our state of spiritual health. President Harold B. Lee noted:

When we see one devoid of respect for himself, as indicated by his conduct, his outward appearance, his speech, and his utter disregard of the basic measures of decency, then certainly we are witnessing the frightening aspect of one over whom Satan has achieved a victory, as the Lord declared he would try to do "to deceive and to blind men, and to lead them captive at his will, . . . to destroy the agency of man." (Moses 4:14.) This is the fate of "even as many as would not hearken unto my voice" (Moses 4:4), so declared the Lord to Moses. (Harold B. Lee, *Stand Ye in Holy Places* [Salt Lake City: Deseret Book Company, 1974], 12)

President Spencer W. Kimball spoke very practically to a generation who had much potential but sent the wrong message by the way they dressed:

Shakespeare had Polonius truly say, "The apparel oft proclaims the man." (*Hamlet,* act 1, sc. 3.) We are affected by our own outward appearances; we tend to fill roles. If we are in our Sunday best, we have little inclination for roughhousing; if we dress for work, we are drawn to work; if we dress immodestly, we are tempted to act immodestly; if we dress like the opposite sex, we tend to lose our sexual identity or some of the graces that distinguish the eternal mission of our sex.

Now, I hope not to be misunderstood: I am *not* saying that you should judge one another by appearance, for that would be folly and worse; I am saying that there is a relationship between how we dress and groom ourselves and how we are inclined to feel and act. . . . We hope that the disregard we sometimes see is mere thoughtlessness and is not deliberate.

Dress suggests our values. How far, we wonder, will men and women go to pay ovations to the god of style? Will men wear rings in their noses when style dictates? Will young people still fall prey to their god of style, which they worship? "Everybody does it."

Tell me: Is it not true that the dress, the grooming, paints an immediate picture and classifies a person? The famous Jerry Rubin says: "Young kids identify short hair with authority, discipline, unhappiness, boredom, hatred of life and long hair with just 'letting go.' Wherever we go, our hair tells people where we stand on Vietnam, lawless campus destructions, and drugs. We're living TV commercials for the revolution. Long hair is the beginning of our liberation from sexual [morality]." What group do you wish to follow and with which group do you wish to identify?

Some young people have prided themselves in wearing the most tattered, soiled, and grubby attire. If we dress in a shabby or sloppy manner, we tend to think and act the same way. I am positive that personal grooming and cleanliness, as well as the clothes we wear, can be tremendous factors in the standards we set and follow on the pathway to immortality and eternal life. (*The Teachings of Spencer W. Kimball,* 379–80)

If you are going to have your foreordained impact on the next generation, you must take into account the way you dress. The world always scorns the cautions and warnings of the living prophets. If we would be wise enough to avoid deception, we should listen and give heed to what they are saying.

Look at your wardrobe. If it needs updating to reflect your newly acquired dedication to righteous living, then start now. You have probably discovered that some of your old CDs and tapes no longer fit in your library, so you may find necessary the cleaning out of your closet. I watch with great interest the appearance of returned missionaries. Within the first six months they label their effectiveness as missionaries and their attitude toward the missions they have just served. One righteous young man or woman can greatly influence an entire ward. Why not be the one? It does matter how you look. The prophets have spoken; now it is up to you whether to follow their counsel and prosper or choose your own way and find out by sad experience that the prophets speak the truth.

9

LETTING THINGS UNFOLD
NATURALLY

HONORABLY RELEASED missionaries often feel the urge to "be perfect right now." But achieving perfection will take much longer than our mortal lifetimes. The Prophet Joseph Smith gave this insightful counsel:

> When you climb up a ladder, you must begin at the bottom, and ascend step by step, until you arrive at the top; and so it is with the principles of the Gospel—you must begin with the first, and go on until you learn all the principles of exaltation. But it will be a great while after you have passed through the veil before you will have learned them. It is not all to be comprehended in this world; it will be a great work to learn our salvation and exaltation even beyond the grave. (Teachings of the Prophet Joseph Smith, 348; italics in original)

To continue to grow without stagnating, create an environment where spiritual growth can continue to occur. Keep out the weeds of a telestial world. Be where you are supposed to be, doing what you are supposed to be doing. The Lord will give you as much as you are capable of receiving as quickly as you are willing. It is *you*, not the Lord, who is impeding your spiritual progress. It is his work and his glory to prepare you for the highest degree of the celestial kingdom; therefore, your slow progress doesn't reflect a lack of desire or capability on his part. We are the ones who impose ceilings and limitations on what we will receive from our Heavenly Father.

We want to pick and choose which commandments to keep and how diligent to be in fulfilling our callings, yet we expect unlimited blessings. Just before his betrayal, the Savior looked longingly back at Jerusalem and lamented, "O Jerusalem, Jerusalem, thou that killest the prophets, and stonest them which are sent unto thee, how often would I have gathered thy children together, even as a hen gathereth her chickens under her wings, and *ye would not!*" (Matthew 23:37; emphasis added). How sad that some individuals try to blame him for their failure to receive promised blessings, when he so willingly offers those blessings.

"Who am I that made man, saith the Lord, that will hold him guiltless that obeys not my commandments? Who am I, saith the Lord, that have promised and have not fulfilled? I command and men obey not; I revoke and they receive not the blessing. Then they say in their hearts: This is not the work of the Lord, for his promises are not fulfilled. But wo unto such, for their reward lurketh beneath, and not from above" (D&C 58:30–33).

Although we hold the key to our spiritual progress and development, we must not "run faster or labor more than [we] have strength" (D&C 10:4; see also Mosiah 4:27). Be patient. The factor determining whether we progress as quickly as we should is the presence or absence of the Spirit. I wish I had understood that better when I was a recently returned missionary. When the Spirit is with us, we are doing all that the Lord expects us to do based on the amount of light and knowledge he has given us. When the Spirit withdraws, we must either repent of whatever has caused the Spirit to leave or take the next step up the ladder of spiritual progress.

It is not important whether others commend our progress. The "spirit of justification" makes all the difference in the world. Trying to force spiritual growth is like trying to force an egg to hatch early or fruit to ripen before its time: "To every thing there is a season, and a time to every purpose under the heaven" (Ecclesiastes 3:1).

Although spiritual lethargy is usually more of a problem than being overzealous, beware of expecting too much too soon. Someday we will have our "calling and election made sure" by receiving the Holy Spirit of Promise. That is certainly a worthy goal, but we must realize it may take years— or more than a lifetime—to accomplish. Enjoy life. Many overenthusiastic returned missionaries become discouraged because those sacred promises have not yet been fulfilled after they have been home six months!

God explained to Abraham that this earth life is a time to be tested and tried in *all things* (see Abraham 3:25). If you consider the implications of that statement, you'll realize that it will take time to experience all the situations in which we can be tried. Marriage and child rearing certainly pose major challenges that you can't possibly experience until you're married and have children! Coping with the normal setbacks of life, solving interpersonal conflicts, and handling unexpected reverses in business, social life, or family affairs all require time to experience. Perhaps that is why the Lord admonishes us to "be still and know that I am God" (D&C 101:16).

Life is somewhat like your mission experience. People will ask you how your mission went. Some will be asking out of courtesy and really won't care to know too many details. Others plan to serve missions themselves and are very interested in your answer. Be honest. Missions are tough. They push you to the limit and then some. It is not a continuous string of blissful, baptizing days. There are problems, health concerns, and difficult companions as well as spiritual experiences and unparalleled highs. If you report that a mission was the easiest time in your life, you are not being completely honest. Although difficult, it was also the most productive time of your life. It was more than worth it! So it is with life. If someone older and more experienced tells you that life is easy, he or she is not being completely honest. You will have challenges. During some periods of extreme difficulty you may wonder how you will ever get through a particular challenge. But somehow you will make it. And like anyone who uses the gospel as the road map through the trials of life, you will agree that life is richly rewarding.

If you expect postmission life to be an unbroken chain of blissful, Spirit-filled days when everything goes your way, you will be very disappointed. Your spiritual muscles were not developed in the mission field by ease. Adversity brought growth. The same is true of life after a mission. Growth comes through continually meeting the challenges of life over a long period of time. When you regularly evaluate your progress, you'll be less likely to be discouraged or to accuse yourself of not making progress.

The temple experience helps you keep life in eternal perspective. Go to the temple when you can enjoy the session without being hurried. Study the symbolic nature of the endowment and let your understanding unfold naturally as the Lord sees fit.

Growth in the mission field occurred subtly, and so will your continued spiritual progress. If you were wise while you were on your mission, you kept a detailed record of your feelings and the events that influenced you. If you are wise now, you will continue to keep a journal. It is beneficial to look back in your journal and reread entries made a year ago, five years ago, or, as you grow older, twenty years ago. You may be surprised at the progress you are making.

Spirituality is a process, not an event. Sanctification is a process, not an event. Earning your exaltation is a process, not an event. Being closer to your goal today than you were last week, understanding the temple endowment better this time, gaining insights into the scriptures that escaped you before, controlling your temper better—all these constitute the progress that makes the process an enjoyable experience. Enjoy the process—and don't rush it!

10

....

COLLEGE ATHLETICS

MANY RETURNING MISSIONARIES consider the issue of whether to play a college sport. If you didn't participate in college athletics before your mission, you are probably not inclined to start participating now. For many who did play college sports, the issue is a much more serious one. During their missions or after returning home, many missionaries have sought counsel on whether to play ball or just focus on finishing school. There isn't a right or wrong answer.

Count the cost. As a missionary you were taught to be goal oriented. Hours of proselyting, numbers of projected baptisms, and deadlines for memorizing discussions and the scriptures were all part of your regular schedule. In order to accomplish any goal, you needed to assess your resources and establish a time frame for accomplishing your goal. The same is true with sports. A certain amount of time is required for physical conditioning, practice, and participation in a sport. Since the Lord doesn't expand the day to meet your desires, you are constrained to play within the "24-hours-a-day" limit that God imposed. Like it or not, when you give twenty hours a week to a sport, there are twenty fewer hours to use in some other activity. That doesn't make sports good or bad; it just makes them time-consuming. If you decide that you want to play no matter what, then the time requirement won't make much difference.

In addition to the time required to practice and play, there will be the scheduling difficulties and road trips. If you marry before you complete college, will your travel schedule pose a hardship on your spouse and children?

Another important consideration is the possibility of Sunday play. If you plan to play professional ball, you can be assured that Sunday play will be required. Before you make a final decision, seek the counsel of your local priesthood leaders and, if possible, talk to a professional athlete who is a member of the Church. By far the most important consideration is "Will I be able to maintain my spirituality in a professional sports environment?" If you cannot answer yes, you may have made your decision already.

If you choose to participate in intramural sports, remember that during your mission you have not been accustomed to training and playing. It is easy to expect the same from yourself as before, even though you are not as fit physically. Ease into competitive sports. Injuries may result when you play too hard before you're physically ready. In fact, you should consider the likelihood of injury as you evaluate any possible career in sports.

Another consideration is more crucial than conditioning—temper control. If you can't control your temper, don't play! Many testimonies have been weakened, feelings hurt, and friendships ended because of uncontrolled tempers. Is it worth it? As members of the Church we are to "stand as witnesses of God at all times and in all things, and in all places that ye may be in, even until death" (Mosiah 18:9). The witness you bear will be for one team or the other—you can't escape that. You may think that no one is watching. Wrong!

On more than a few occasions, my sons have come home from Church activities and reported on the conduct of Brother So-and-so.

In time, your role will shift from participant to spectator. Learning how to be a good spectator can be equally challenging. You don't have to argue or fight with the Cub Scout leader if your son's pinewood derby car doesn't win first place! You don't have to fight with or bully the Pony League coach if your son doesn't get to play all the time. Learning how to control yourself during times of intense competition is a "must" if you desire to progress until you become like your Heavenly Father. You are never justified in losing your temper at a ball game. If you can't control yourself, avoid the situation. The rewards for controlling yourself include greater peace of mind and conscience and more joy in life.

Physical fitness is important. There may come a time, however, when due to accident or illness you are physically challenged. In fact, that may already be the case. Some of the most influential people in my life are people who have not had the use of either their arms or their legs. Learning to live with physical disabilities can cause you to shine. Learning to make the best of your circumstances, whatever they are, certainly puts you in a favorable position for future judgment.

11

....

VISITING YOUR MISSION AREA

MISSIONARIES WHO LEARN TO serve with all their "heart, might, mind, and strength" will learn to love the people more than they ever dreamed possible. Some missionaries report that they love their investigators more than they love members of their own families. You may even have met someone in your mission area who seemed absolutely wonderful, someone with whom you could easily fall in love. While you were serving your mission, you recognized the absolute necessity of suppressing all romantic interest in that person. But now perhaps you have the idea that you would like to return to the area and date her or him.

Whether or not you are romantically interested in someone in your mission area, it is natural to want to come back and visit after your formal mission is complete. If you served in a foreign country, returning after your mission is more difficult. If you served closer to home, it is easier to return to your field of labor.

One of the discoveries missionaries make when they return home is that the mantle of a missionary is taken from them when their stake president officially releases them. This mantle is an indefinable but very real feeling of stewardship, responsibility, and heightened spiritual awareness regarding matters pertaining to missionary work. Try as you will, the feelings you experience when you revisit your mission will not be the same as when you served there. The members may still warmly greet you, those you helped convert will still love you, and other missionaries may still remember you, but it will be different.

Particularly if you served in a foreign country or among a people who were not well versed in the gospel, you may find that the people still consider you a missionary when you return to visit your former area. Therein lies the danger. If you should decide to socialize with or date someone from that area, the people may become confused. They may wonder why a "missionary" is dating their daughter or son. Unless your experience is entirely different from that of missions I have observed, your dating someone in your former mission area will have a negative impact on missionary work there. In three separate cities and within three different cultures, the work came to a screeching halt when elders returned and started dating girls from those cultures.

It is difficult to understand why dedicated missionaries would date people who were in their missions when they know the negative impact their behavior will have on the work. Why would you want to undo in one day what you have worked two years or eighteen months to build? Such actions negatively affect the work of those who have gone before and those who are still serving.

In one particular city the average weekly church attendance dropped from seventy to two after a returned missionary came back to the area, dated a native girl, and then dropped her when he realized they were not right for each other. In our culture it is acceptable to date different people and to discontinue dating when things are not going right. But in many other cultures, dating is a serious prelude to marriage and is not discontinued without disgrace to the girl and her family in the eyes of the entire culture.

Of course there isn't a law that states you can't date those you worked with, but I would strongly discourage it. For your entire mission you were there not to do your will but the will of him who sent you. Why would you want to change after completing a successful mission?

If you are working among the English-speaking population in the United States, then returning to date may not have such a negative impact. However, as you take your date to church, if you are sensitive, you may still notice the raising of eyebrows and the furrowing of brows as indications of disapproval or questioning. It just never felt right when former missionaries came back to date and associate with the members and missionaries in a capacity that cast a questioning shadow over the work in which other missionaries were still engaged.

When you first go home, there is going to be a period of adjustment. Many times you may experience homesickness for your mission. If you return to the area within the first three or four months after your release, you may be reacting to that homesickness. Instead, consider staying home for six or eight months before deciding to return. Chances are you will have found your niche at home by then, and your desire to return may have lessened even though you will always love the people you served. Use these months to get things into perspective, and then if you still choose to return, you will not be viewed as a recently released missionary. The companion you were serving with in your last area will probably have been transferred. The memory of you as a missionary will have faded. The negative impact will not be as great as it would have been just a few months after your release.

However, be aware that the cultural barriers, if any, will still be just as strong as ever.

As you reflect on your mission, you may experience the "grass is always greener on the other side of the fence" syndrome. When you return to your area, it won't be quite as beautiful as you remember it. The people will not be quite as celestial as you remember them being. You could easily be very disappointed if you return. Many missionaries have chosen to remember the mission the way they left it rather than return and destroy their image of it.

There is another consideration in dating someone you met on your mission. He or she knew you when you were a missionary. Although you want to maintain the same dynamic personality, the intensity with which you live life after your mission will be different. If you were the missionary you were called to be, your entire focus was on spiritual things. As you return home, it isn't even desirable that you stay totally focused on spiritual things. You must find a job, get back into school, accept a position in the Church, start a social life, and start working toward your life's career. That balance of your social, physical, intellectual, and spiritual sides (see Luke 2:52) is a must if you are going to be like the Savior.

Too often girls and guys fall in love with full-time missionaries, who are focused entirely on spiritual things, only to find they are not what they expected or wanted when the physical, social, and intellectual factors are considered. If you return within a month or two of your release, you are still in the adjustment stage. The person you are dating in the mission area may still not be able to get a true picture of what you will be like. Think of the heartache for both of you if you marry and later find you are not compatible.

If you are totally honest with yourself, you will know whether you are violating good judgment by returning to the mission area. Make it a matter of prayer, and listen for the guidance of the Spirit before you take off for the area where you served your mission. Talk to your parents and even to your bishop if you still feel confused. They see things with a broad perspective that may not be available to you right now.

If after doing these things you still feel you should return to your mission area, be honest with yourself, once you arrive, in evaluating whether or not you should have come. How can you tell? If you find yourself sneaking around, avoiding the mission president or mission leaders, or asking members and nonmembers not to mention to the full-time missionaries that you are in the area, then common sense tells you that you shouldn't be there. Do you have to visit the mission president while you are there? No, not at all. But if you fear that he'll find out you are in the area, be honest enough to realize you shouldn't be there. Then go home and get on with your life.

If you decide, after a reasonable length of time, to go back to visit or date in your former mission area, avoid dressing like the full-time missionaries. If the only thing that distinguishes you from the missionaries is your lack of a name tag, people start to wonder. Have the full-time missionaries just taken off their name tags? Should they report you to the mission president? How can they distinguish you from the real elders or sisters? These are just a few of the questions I fielded as a mission president. It was difficult to explain that the individuals who came back were no longer missionaries and I no longer had a stewardship over them.

Once you arrive in your former area of labor, be careful about spending too much time with the missionaries who are still serving. They have work to do, and you won't want to hold them back in any way. If you want to visit, team up with, or participate in companion exchanges (commonly called splits) with the full-time missionaries, get permission from the mission president. He may not mind your spending some time with them. On the other hand, he may have very strong feelings about it, because your mere presence will cause the missionaries to think about the end of their missions. If you could see the negative impact of visits from recently returned missionaries, you would think twice about visiting the missionaries who are still serving. If there had been many positive experiences of missionaries coming back to visit, I would give you different advice. But in my view, the risk you take of becoming a deterrent to the work is not worth fleeting happiness that comes from being there when you really shouldn't.

If you do return to visit, make the visit short and leave while the people still want you to stay. You will remember the poverty of so many families who gave their all to feed the missionaries. Moving in with or imposing on a family you helped convert may be met with smiles and gratitude, but it may also cause the collapse of their monthly budget. Be sensitive to the economic impact on the people you visit.

Very few people just sit around waiting for your visit. Call in advance and let them know you will be in the area and ask if they would be available for a short visit. Be very sensitive to the demands on the mission president's time. He and his wife will probably be glad to see you, but remember, they still have a calling that requires almost twenty-four hours a day, seven days a week to fulfill. A short, planned thirty-minute visit is much more appreciated than an unannounced two-hour visit.

By using the same sensitivity you developed while on your mission, you will be able to make your visit more pleasant and worthwhile, and your presence will not be as troublesome as it has been when missionaries have thought only of themselves rather than the continuing progress of the work. The Lord will bless you to know the right thing to do.

12

BEING FRIENDS WITHOUT COMPROMISING

WHEN YOU RETURN HOME AFTER your mission, rejoining your old social group may pose some unique challenges— depending on your focus before your mission. Many elders and sisters approach their former friends with a justifiable sense of fear. If your friends supported you in keeping the commandments, then returning to their social circle will not be difficult. If your friends chose not to go on missions, they may still be focused on things that seem unimportant or almost disgusting to you now. They may still be worried about who is dating their old boyfriend or girlfriend, where the big party is for this weekend, who has the fastest car, or who has had the latest brush with the law.

One elder came to an interview a couple of months before the end of his mission carrying a letter he had received from a friend. His friend described the parties they were planning for him, the girl they were priming for his "welcome home," and the assortment of booze they were arranging to have at the party. The elder was concerned about how he could keep their friendship without compromising his standards. We talked frankly for a long time.

We talked about how his friends would be excited to have

him back. The party would go really well until it came his turn to demonstrate his allegiance to them by drinking or getting involved with the girl. When he refused, the tension would rise. His continued refusal to lower his standards would perhaps at first be seen by his friends as an obstacle they could overcome in time. They might strengthen their pleas to him to be "one of the crowd." When they failed to lure him back into his old ways, his friends would begin to draw away from him. He would eventually have to decide whether to go with the guys or stay true to his testimony. I asked him to write and let me know how things went. A couple of months after his release came his letter. He outlined the struggles in trying to convert his less-active member friends to his newly discovered lifestyle. He recounted the verbal abuse and teasing he had taken. He outlined the very situations we had talked about and ended the letter by telling about the new set of friends he was developing. He wrote how sorry he felt to have to decide between his friends and the Church. His testimony at the end of the letter confirming how good it felt to make right choices reinforced my faith in the ability of youth to make righteous decisions.

Before you leave the mission field, decide how to handle sticky social situations. What are you going to do if your friends throw a party for you and everyone wants to watch an R-rated video? Can you use humor to soften your refusal to watch? You might say, "I don't think my mom would let me watch this!" Laughter may result, but others may suggest that you play a game rather than watch the video. If you are not firm in your refusal, they will push you to the limit. If they insist on watching the video, you might say something like, "I don't want to make you guys uncomfortable, but I promised myself I wouldn't watch R-rated movies. Tell me how long it will last and I'll be back when it's over."

Today's culture seems oriented towards watching videos. Decide before you lose the missionary mantle what you will watch and what you will not. Make that decision only once. You surely have become realistic enough to realize that you cannot feed your mind on telestial food and expect celestial thoughts. Very few videos and movies today promote virtue, goodness, service, true Christlike love, and devotion to a higher cause. You are only deceiving yourself if you rationalize that movies, songs, and lyrics have no effect on your thoughts and spirituality. Feed your mind and spirit on celestial materials and you will see how much easier it is to avoid telestial temptations.

If you associated with a rowdy group before your mission and if there is the slightest possibility that they will try to lace your drink with alcohol, make sure that when you are with them you drink from a can of pop that you open yourself. Be on guard until you have established a social group where alcohol and drugs are not even used.

It is easy to stay straight if you never take the first step off the track. Well-defined guidelines will make your social reentry much easier. Make yourself a list of "these things I will do" and another list of "these things I will not do." You have paid a tremendous price to get where you are now; to return to the old ways would be like going to four years of college only to work in a fast-food restaurant. Trying to "return" is a mark of a lack of mature understanding. The world is not the same place as when you left. If you are unconvinced, watch an evening of television! You will likely be shocked. Having been away from television for eighteen months or two years, you will not have been desensitized into accepting filth as normal. You may even rent a movie you liked before your mission only to turn it off unwatched, finding that it contains much more offensive material than you had realized. You cannot possibly return to the environment you left two years ago, because it no longer exists. Your less-active friends may be doing the same things they did before your mission, but there is no stagnation in life. They will actually be further away from their eternal goals than they were when you left.

Can you be a factor for change among your friends? Certainly. But be careful not to try to influence the whole rowdy group at once; if you tackle several friends who are off the track, their combined influence may overpower your desire to do good and you may join them. Pick the friend who is most likely to change, and do things with him or her. If you notice yourself being strongly tempted to slip into old ways you have put behind you, pull away from your less-active friends until you are strong enough to influence them instead of the other way around.

Once you have "converted" one friend to live a more righteous life, then the two of you can tackle another friend. Certainly their souls are as important to save as the souls of the investigators you worked with your whole mission. Just be aware that it is sometimes more difficult to rekindle the fire of testimony after it has been doused with the ice water of sin than it is to start a testimony fire from dry wood. Don't be discouraged. If you are successful, your friends will one day thank you for saving their spiritual lives.

You will probably notice that your whole approach to social life has changed since returning from your mission. Life has a more serious meaning. There is more to life than just play and fun. Your desire for conversation with some substance rather than just gossip may surprise your former friends. Going on dates will still be fun, but you will probably be oriented toward finding someone you could marry rather than just having a good time. You may discover that hanging out gets old in a hurry. You will probably want something more fulfilling and challenging. All of these feelings are natural and desirable.

Your mission has cast you forever into a leadership role. Take the challenge to throw the best parties, plan the most fun dates, be the most original person around. Being creative requires a lot more energy, but once you have developed the reputation, others will want to join you. When you plan the parties, you can set the standards for the activities. People will gladly meet the qualifications if the parties are fun.

That will be your challenge. Take charge in a positive way. Let people see the true and lasting fun that comes when you can remember not only the party but after the party as well. Make it your job to bring out the best in others. If you need some ideas for fun, creative dates, see the list in the back of the book for inexpensive but memory-creating activities.

13

STARTING TO DATE AGAIN

LISTENING TO ELDERS' AND SISTERS' dating worries is one of the most humorous parts of the exit interview. It was humorous to me as a mission president, not to them! Dating is a very real concern after having been away for eighteen months or two years.

For young men who either do not have anyone waiting or no longer have anyone waiting, the question is, "How do I start dating again without fulfilling the reputation of a returned missionary?" For those who are not aware of the unfortunate definition of a returned missionary, it is "an octopus with a testimony"! I really don't know for sure that the reputation is correct, but that's the perception some young ladies have of some young men who are returned missionaries. Who knows? That definition may even fit a few overeager returned sister missionaries.

Among those of you who have recently returned from a mission, it is not uncommon to feel uncomfortable when you are alone with a member of the opposite sex. You may also feel you are compromising your virtue if you hold hands. That sounds really silly, but judging from the reports of missionaries who have gone through the experience, I feel I should warn you to be prepared for those feelings if they crop up. Even mission presidents have some adjusting to do when they first arrive home. At our "welcome home" gathering, which many of our returned missionaries attended (some with dates), I had to restrain myself from standing up and telling all those beautiful young women and handsome young men to move farther away from my missionaries! For three years I had done everything in my power to help the missionaries keep their distance from attractive members of the opposite sex; now here they were holding hands, arms around each other, and looking very much in love. It took a few minutes for me to realize that many of them were now husbands and wives!

When you first return home, consider going on group dates or at least double dating for the first few times. If you have spoken a different language for the past several months, conversing in English may be a real challenge. It reduces stress when more people are there to share the burden of conversation. Even if you're sure you know all about dating, it is comforting to watch another couple interact to reinforce your behavior.

Should you begin each date with prayer? Yes, but probably not with your date! Prayer, as you know, is a very intimate experience. Too many intimate experiences early in the dating process can lead to serious problems later. Pray alone before you go on a date. Then conduct yourself properly during your date so that when you return home, your prayer of reporting to your Heavenly Father will be an enjoyable experience. Save the experience of praying together for that time in the future when casual dating becomes serious courtship. Would you be violating some Church standard if you pray with your date? No. The choice is yours and certainly must be subject to whatever the Spirit prompts you to do.

Eternity is a long time. Relationships must be allowed to develop slowly. Consider the problem of getting engaged within a couple of weeks of getting home—especially to a person who has not waited for you. When you return home, the mantle of a missionary is still on your shoulders. When you are released and that mantle is removed, you still enjoy lingering blessings—and you may still feel more like a missionary than like a fiancé. Give yourself time to readjust to your "civilian" personality, the new "real you"—not a less spiritual you, but nevertheless a different person than you were the moment you stepped off the plane from your mission. Sometimes it takes a month or two before the real you emerges. If you are engaged or married before this readjustment occurs, it will cause real stress in your marriage as your spouse tries to reconcile the new you with the person they thought they were marrying. The "Courtship" section of this book offers suggestions on how to really get to know each other before marriage.

Continuing with the idea of letting your relationship develop slowly, be sure that physical involvement does not violate your resolve to maintain spirituality. The reputation talked about earlier suggests that some returned missionaries want to make up for lost time. Inappropriate or excessive physical intimacy not only scares your date but demonstrates a lack of self-control and causes a drastic loss in your spirituality. Before you leave the mission field, and before you are confronted with a highly charged emotional situation, determine what kissing means to you. Is it a mere expression of affection or is it a demonstration of true love? Is kissing something you do with everyone you go out with, or is it something special that is only shared with someone you hope to marry? You must decide based on your newly acquired vision of who you are and what you have the potential of becoming.

You may have questions about "making out"—extended kissing and hugging. You may wonder how much is too much. Decide now, before you get into any romantic situations, to behave in ways that will help your thoughts stay pure. Review the Church's pamphlet *For the Strength of Youth* in order to make certain you understand exactly what is and is not appropriate. Don't be afraid to ask a parent or trusted priesthood leader questions about moral purity.

If your date feels he or she has to be on guard, you need to reevaluate the message you are sending. When you take control of the dating environment, it is much easier to control your behavior. Video parties pose a greater risk of increased physical intimacy than do volleyball parties or board games.

Do you have to return to the dating scene immediately? No, that is a personal choice. But Church leaders have cautioned about waiting too long before beginning your search for a spouse. Focusing too much on meeting your own needs while ignoring your God-given responsibilities makes you increasingly insensitive to the Spirit. Although you may feel that you have plenty of time, the years will fly by very quickly. The window for marriage is a little larger than the window for serving a mission, but not by much. A mission's window is from age nineteen to twenty-six for a young man. Only rarely can a person go before reaching age nineteen, and only by special permission can a person go after age twenty-six. Marriage age does not have General Authority restrictions like a mission, but it does have some practical limitations. The ideal marriage window for young men in the United States seems to be from age twenty-one to age thirty.

Yes, there are those who marry before age twenty-one if they choose not to serve missions. There are also young men who wait until after they are thirty to marry, but the selection of potential spouses and your appeal as a mate may diminish greatly after you reach age thirty.

Postponing marriage until schooling is complete, employment is secured, or fun has been experienced may sound good now, but this course of action may bring sorrow in the future. You may have toured the world with your friends, but you won't be living with them for the rest of your life. Shared experiences as husband and wife are among life's richest blessings. Many young couples have expressed their thankfulness for not waiting until later to be married. Financial challenges may crop up for young married couples, but the rewards of marriage eclipse the inconvenience and expense.

Do you have to get married within six months of being released? Certainly not. Seldom, if ever, will a mission president set a time limit on such an important decision. On your mission, you learned to say, "Father, . . . not my will, but thine, be done" (Luke 22:42). Why change now? It would be foolish to expect to marry in six months if your future mate was not to come within your circle of acquaintances for two years! It is equally unwise to wait for six months if the Spirit directs you to get married immediately! Six months, two months, or two years—time is not the issue. When the Spirit prompts you to make the move toward marriage, make it! Following the guidance of the Spirit is of primary importance. Remember that "the Spirit knoweth all things" (Alma 7:13) and will never lead you astray. The Lord's timing may not be according to your timetable, but it will always be correct.

For those who have someone special waiting, the challenges will be different but just as real. Some missionaries who have sweethearts waiting feel an obligation to marry them. After all, this person has waited faithfully for a long time. However, it is not unusual for missionaries to change dramatically during their missions. Unless the person at home has made similar strides, you may find that you are not as interested in that person as you were before your mission. You may agree to date for a while before setting a wedding date. If either of you has reservations after dating for a while, date other people before making a decision of such eternal consequence.

Within a month of his return from his mission, a friend of mine, who had served an honorable mission, married the girl who had waited for him. Soon after, they divorced. Both he and his former wife are great people. A lot of heartache and disappointment could have been prevented if they had taken the Lord's advice to "be still and know that I am God" (D&C 101:16). Take your time. If your love is eternal, it will wait for a few months until the dust has settled. Plans and preparation take time. Rushing the most important decision you will ever make is hardly a manifestation of spiritual maturity.

If things don't work out, break off the relationship gently and without bitter feelings. It may be that now isn't the right time, but later on might be. Even if things never work out between you, why create an enemy of one who has been a close friend?

Do people wait for missionaries and have everything work out? Sure, all the time. What a blessing to have shared such a sustained spiritual experience with that special someone who becomes your eternal companion. My sister waited for her missionary, and they now have a wonderful marriage and family. Many others have done the same thing. The key is to continue to include the Lord in your dating, courtship, and marriage the way you included him in your missionary activity.

14

......

Social Sensitivity

Many lessons you learned on your mission will enrich your postmission life as you continue to apply them. A few of those lessons will be emphasized in this chapter to remind you of proper social etiquette.

Know when to leave. Do you remember the mission counsel to make your visits brief, always leaving with the people wanting you to stay longer? That is good advice at home, too. You will probably want to visit people who have positively influenced you. They will want you to visit. But remember to plan ahead by telephoning and asking when it would be convenient for them to chat for a few minutes. If you just drop in, then consider using the rule of thumb you applied when visiting members to get a drink of water or a referral—stay fifteen to twenty minutes maximum.

How can you tell if people want you to stay longer? After fifteen minutes you might say something like, "Well, I need to be going. It's been great to visit with you." If the people you are visiting really want you to stay longer, they will protest your leaving and invite you to stay for dinner or just to visit longer. Then feel free to stay. If they thank you for coming and encourage you to come again, you can know for sure that it's time to go.

If you want to spend more time with someone, call and

set an appointment. If your mission president has returned from his mission and lives nearby, he will no doubt enjoy visiting with you. We are busy people, but we love to have returned missionaries from our mission come by and visit. If they call, we will generally invite them over for dinner! Everybody wins then. We get to visit with people we love, and they get to enjoy good home cooking.

If you're invited to dinner, remember the mission rule to limit dinner appointments to one hour or so unless there is a special purpose. Staying all evening would probably make your host a little uncomfortable.

On your mission you learned to be sensitive to local customs. Manners may vary from country to country, but you tried to adjust to the expectations of your host. The same thing applies when visiting others after you return home. Put on your best manners. Manners indicate a spiritually mature individual. "Please," "thank you," and "excuse me" are not difficult words, but they certainly set you apart from thoughtless crowds who consider only their own needs.

President David O. McKay used to stand every time Sister McKay entered the room. We can follow his example by similarly honoring others, by performing small, courteous acts, and by generously expressing our appreciation for our host and hostess.

It is important to show proper respect for others as we converse with them. Learning to listen and not interrupt is difficult, especially if you have something important to say, but it pays great dividends. It automatically labels you as a courteous person. Listening also happens to be the only way you can learn that other people really do have important things to say.

In your mission area, you tried to build relationships

based on beliefs you and your investigator had in common. When dealing with people at home, it is easy to focus on differences and on their weaknesses. However, it is more Christlike to accentuate the positive traits you see in them. You are no longer in the same ministerial position to call people to repentance. People often accuse returned missionaries of being critical of everything that is different from what they're used to. The food you like is not scripturally superior to the food others may prefer. The entertainment you enjoy and the kind of music you prefer do not necessarily have the divine stamp of approval. You are not the measuring stick against which all activities are judged. Allow people to have their own likes and dislikes. You are not obliged to comment on every subject. Pizza happens to be a food I don't like, but that doesn't mean I should insist that everyone avoid eating pizza. Do you tend to treat your own personal likes and dislikes as a standard for everyone else? If you do, practice being more accepting and less vocal.

It may not be right, but you cannot avoid being socially labeled if you associate with the wrong crowd. It is noble to try to fellowship the wayward, but you always run the risk of giving people the impression that you are one of them. Whether you care to admit it or not, the clothes you wear also send a powerful message about how you view yourself.

As a teacher for many years and also as the president of a company, I had multiple occasions to interact with students and other people who were seeking promotions or employment. A neatly dressed person projects a positive message. I tried to avoid labeling people because of their appearance, but I was more likely to hire a person who looked trustworthy than one who took no thought for their appearance. I have asked numerous business leaders how they view a job applicant's appearance. They all confirmed the truth of this principle. If you want a job, look like you want it.

You made sacred covenants before entering the mission field. If your wardrobe at home makes it impossible for you to properly wear temple garments, you need to change your wardrobe. Your commitment to continued spirituality is called into question by priesthood leaders and members when you disregard the covenants you made in the temple. There will certainly be times when you will remove the garment. Very active sports such as basketball, swimming parties, and possibly a few other activities would suggest the appropriateness of going without garments. When you seek for opportunities to wear them rather than remove them, your spiritual understanding begins to shine through. Sunbathing, mowing the lawn without a shirt on, and going around all day in athletic shorts when not required send a message. Live your testimony.

On your mission, people served you. They invited you to dinner and included you in family outings. It is easy to fall into the trap of expecting these things after your mission. If you expect to be served, you may become bitter when it doesn't happen. It is much easier to *expect nothing!* If no one invites you over to eat, that is all right. If no one thanks you for serving a mission, that won't rattle your testimony. If people totally ignore you (which they won't!), that isn't a reason for becoming less active in the Church.

Look at the positive side of not expecting anything. Whenever anyone gives you a gift, invites you to dinner, or includes you in a family outing, you are overflowing with gratitude. That is the way it should be. Be grateful for everything people do for you. How much more at rest you will feel when you expect to make your own way rather than expecting someone else to pave the way for you.

None of us has arrived at perfection yet. Overcoming socially unacceptable behavior is a positive goal. Be aware of how your speech and actions affect those around you. If others send nonverbal (or verbal!) cues that suggest their disapproval, consider what you are doing or saying and see if they are alerting you to something that will have to be overcome before you will be welcome in the celestial kingdom. Just as you did on your mission, be humble and teachable enough to take corrective advice from anyone who cares enough to give it. There will be those who desire to see you fail. Some may even sense a divinely given mission to help you experience reality. Consider comments and act on them according to their merit, not the advice-giver's motive, and continue the perfecting process.

You will probably find that postmission social experiences take on an entirely different meaning. Everything before the mission may have been fun and games. After the mission you may find you are more interested in getting on with life. You will still have fun and still play games, but behind all of the frivolity will be more seriousness and looking to the future.

It is much easier to be straight when everyone in your social circle is straight. While you were serving your mission you were probably acutely aware of how people considered you a role model for their children and for themselves. Things have not changed. You will forever be labeled as a "returned missionary." It is your responsibility to set an example throughout your life. A clear understanding of this responsibility will be yet another incentive to live the way you know you should live. What a joy you will be to your parents and what a credit you will be to yourself when you no longer depend on someone else to control your behavior. Even when you are not being supervised, do you act in an acceptable way? Have you completely shed the childish attitude of trying to "get away with" things? Could you with confidence invite the Savior to participate in your social activities? These and many similar questions will help you govern yourself socially when you return.

There will probably be awkward situations. Everything may not run smoothly. There may be experiences that require you to stretch beyond the principles you learned on your mission. But your mission will give you the headstart you need to ensure that, socially speaking, you don't just wander aimlessly.

15

BALANCING BRAIN AND BRAWN

WHAT WILL YOU DO WITH THE rest of your life? That sounds like such a large, all-encompassing question. It is, and for that reason you owe it to yourself to make the decision deliberately, taking whatever time it requires to decide wisely. There isn't necessarily a right or wrong answer concerning your future. In order to determine the direction your life will take, however, you will want to find honest answers to some practical questions. For many the decision to return to school was made before they served a mission. Others worked for the year or so following high school to earn enough money to partially pay for the mission. Still others have no real desire to pursue academic careers. The first question you may want to ask yourself is "Do I know what I want to be in life?" You may feel a great sense of alarm when you realize that you are less sure now of what you ultimately want to become than you were before you started your mission. That isn't unusual, nor is it undesirable. When missionaries met together as part of the exit process from our mission each month, we would ask them to show by the raise of their hands if they knew exactly what they wanted to be or if their plans were more definite now than before their mission. It was not unusual for only one or two or even no hands to be raised.

After a good laugh, we would discuss how to decide, and we'd mention that they may change their minds several times before finally settling on a chosen career. As you dream about the future, do you have at least an area where you visualize yourself? Does that profession or career require a college degree or perhaps even graduate schooling? If an advanced degree is required in your chosen field, don't try to rewrite the requirements because you don't want to go to school or because you are sick of studying and taking classes. If you are going back to run the farm, advanced schooling may not seem necessary until you look at the high-tech world in which you live. It may require more specialized training to compete in agriculture than you think it will. Talk to people who are on the cutting edge of your chosen profession. Be careful in taking too much advice from people who freely counsel without much personal experience.

Elder John H. Groberg of the First Quorum of the Seventy gave some timely advice on how to make decisions about your future:

> In the past I have tried to figure out whether I should go into business or into teaching or into the arts or whatever. As I have begun to proceed along one path, having more or less gathered what facts I could, I have found that if that decision was wrong or was taking me down the wrong path—not necessarily an evil one, but one that was not right for me—without fail, the Lord has always let me know just this emphatically: "That is wrong; do not go that way. That is not for you!"
>
> On the other hand, there may have been two or three ways that I could have gone, any one of which would have been right and would have been in the general

area providing the experience and means whereby I could fulfill the mission that the Lord had in mind for me. Because he knows we need the growth, he generally does not point and say, "Open that door and go twelve yards in that direction; then turn right and go two miles . . . " But if it is wrong, he will let us know—we will feel it for sure. I am positive of that. So rather than saying, "I will not move until I have this burning in my heart," let us turn it around and say, "I will move, unless I feel it is wrong; and if it is wrong, then I will not do it." By eliminating all of these wrong courses, very quickly you will find yourself going in the direction that you ought to be going, and then you can receive the assurance: "Yes, I am going in the right direction. I am doing what my Father in Heaven wants me to do because I am not doing the things he does not want me to do." And you can know that for sure. That is part of the growth process and part of accomplishing what our Father in Heaven has in mind for us. ("What Is Your Mission?" *Speeches of the Year, 1979* [Provo: Brigham Young University Press, 1980], 97–98)

If you do not know what you want to do with the rest of your life, how can you find out? At universities, colleges, and employment centers in most cities, you can take free aptitude tests that indicate your interests and abilities. These tests won't tell you to be a telemarketing specialist. They might say that people who have likes and dislikes similar to yours excel in careers that include sales—then they may list a dozen careers. It is likely that you will want to learn more about several of the careers listed. Of course, you might look through the suggestions and decide that none of them holds much appeal for you. It will at least be a beginning place.

You may want to shop around and talk to people in various professions. Most professional people will gladly talk to you about their careers. Being a doctor holds a lot of appeal to the unrealistic because of the high wages and the social status. If you want to become a doctor, talk to some doctors about the number of years of schooling required as well as the demands on their time when they are established. If you want to be a doctor, that's wonderful, but go into it with your eyes open.

A friend of mind has great advice for people who want to know what they should do with their lives. He asks them to write down three things they would like to do with their lives if money were not a consideration. After the three things are listed, he has them circle their first choice. "Now," he says, "go out and find a way to have people pay you for doing what you love most!" Sounds so simple. He is a great example of what he preaches. He explains that you want to spend your life doing something you really love doing. Imagine looking forward to each day of work. Contrast that with the dread most people feel as they go to work and count the months until vacation or the days until the weekend or the next holiday. What a way to spend life—wishing the next day would never come. Yet millions of people do that every day. My friend's philosophy is "Yes, but not for money! Yes, I will go to work because I love what I am doing and want to make an impact, not merely because it pays good money." Think strongly about that. If you find yourself in a job you hate, why not change? Your life will not fall apart if you change. Recently I heard a follow-up report on college graduates. Within two years of graduation, eighty percent of these highly trained college graduates are working in careers outside their majors.

You may think that you can't afford to change majors if you are partway through your educational career. Perhaps you can't afford not to! With just one life to live, don't you think it is worth doing something that you really want to do? My friend loves traveling, meeting people, and tackling difficult problems. He is president and CEO of his own public relations firm. He loves his job and is paid well for doing it. I love teaching. I have strong convictions and do not like to apologize for my beliefs. I really like young people and enjoy being challenged to show how the gospel principles apply to life. So I teach religion! I can hardly wait to get to class every day to see what new challenges await me. I am actually paid for doing what I love most! The same could be said of construction workers, bankers, doctors, lawyers, or people in any other profession. In each of these professions there are individuals who love their work. There are also those who hate their work. Jobs, careers, and professions are neither inherently exciting or boring; they are what your attitude makes them.

You may profit by reading your patriarchal blessing for hints or clues on what you should do. One young man came up to me after a class in which we had discussed patriarchal blessings. Smiling, he told me that his blessing said he would use his body to earn a living. He had always thought that meant he was going to be a ditch digger. Now he is being recruited as a professional football player. He liked that interpretation much better. Your blessing may not explicitly say you should be a dentist or a teacher. It may suggest that you will work with people or that your contribution will be mainly in bringing forth new ideas and technology. I wanted to be a forest ranger. But the wording in my patriarchal blessing directed me toward teaching the gospel. After more than twenty-five years of professional teaching, I can't imagine being anything other than a teacher.

Whatever career you choose, make sure that your chosen work will satisfy your needs now and in the future and that it is honorable. What sounds like big money to you now may not be enough to support your family later if you do not plan for a career that includes growth opportunities. Many people have decided to take high-paying jobs rather than continue their education and are now struggling to keep up with the financial demands of their families. On the other hand, many of those who have chosen to continue with their education have struggled during the college years but are reaping financial benefits now. Money is not everything, but it is certainly easier to cope with life's other problems when financial woes are not a constant threat.

Do you have to go to college to be successful? No, unless your chosen career requires a diploma. It is really difficult to be satisfied when you deserve a promotion or a raise and someone else gets it because they have a degree and you don't. You may believe that the most qualified applicant always gets the job. I wish that were true. More often than not, it is the person with the college degree or other credentials who gets his or her name on the office door. Ask any number of very skilled workers who lack the degree and you may be overwhelmed at their response. Don't expect equity and fairness in the workplace until the millennial day.

We have considered the negative effects of not having the necessary credentials. You must also realize that too much education may also close some doors. You might be overprepared for a job. A custodian with a doctor's degree might sound funny to you. You might say, "Well, if I want to be a custodian, can't I have a degree?" Yes, but there may be other problems. You may be viewed with suspicion by a supervisor who has only a high school education. When you open certain doors, you automatically close others.

16

GETTING EMPLOYMENT
OR JUST A JOB

WHEN YOU FIRST ARRIVE HOME you may worry that you won't be able to find a job. Some people will be fortunate enough to have family members who can employ them. Others will be able to return to the jobs they had before their missions. If you plan to return to school immediately, you will have to go to where the school is located and compete with many others for a job.

You may consider your skills and think that you're seriously lacking. Wait a minute! You have a lot to offer. You have spent the last eighteen months or two years in one of the most highly specialized public relations ventures in the world. You have trained and supervised people, organized programs, and solved complex problems. You have successfully completed a difficult task. You don't have alcohol problems, drug addictions, or problems such as dishonesty or disloyalty. Your appearance is a primary selling tool. Most employers would like to have their entire workforce look like you! You may be fairly fluent in a foreign language. You may know a different culture and customs and have a rapport with the people. This list could go on and on. You need to know that you have a wealth of resources to offer any enterprising employer. Returned missionaries are highly sought after in the business world.

In interviewing a number of potential employers, we compiled the following list of pointers to help you succeed:

1. When you go for the interview, dress as if applying for the position just above the one for which you are actually applying. If you are trying to become a checker or stocker at a grocery store, go dressed like the supervisor of the checkers or stockers. The impression you want to make is that when the supervisory position becomes available, you could be considered. What a subtle little seed to plant for your first major promotion before you even land your job.

2. Look clean and neat. Sloppy people send a negative message. You may be the greatest person in the world, but if you look like you take little or no pride in yourself, someone else will likely be given the job.

3. A cheerful disposition is almost as rare a commodity as an honest employee. A pleasant look, a willingness to look the interviewer in the eye, and the very way you carry yourself sends a powerful message to the person making the hiring decision.

4. If you are leaving one job for another, don't speak ill of your former employer. In the back of your potential employer's mind will be the question of whether you will talk about him or her the same way if things don't work out! Be honest when asked why you are leaving your present job. You might say, "My employer and I don't see eye to eye on several issues." Everyone is entitled to a difference of opinion. Your job hunt will be more successful if you have a positive letter of recommendation from your former employer.

5. You cannot afford to leave any job with a bitter taste in your mouth or their mouth. Sometimes this is more difficult

than you may think. If you have given an honest day's labor for an honest day's pay, you can leave knowing that you have done your best. Use the skills you developed in the mission field to smooth out the rough places between you and your former boss. Give adequate notice before leaving so your employer is not left in a bind. Offer to help find a replacement if you know people who might work out.

6. Be teachable in your new position. As a missionary you have often had to move into a ward or branch, evaluate the state of the missionary program, and make whatever corrections were necessary to get things going again. The temptation is to do that the first week or so on your job. Reread the chapter "Readjusting to Your Family" and follow that counsel as you adjust to a new job. You will have plenty of opportunities later to make suggestions for improvement. Some things must be done in a certain way even though you may be able to see a more efficient way. You may have had experiences in the mission field with a newly arrived missionary who knew all the answers and wanted to rearrange everything. You will recall how irritated you felt. Don't you make the same mistake as a "greeny" at home or at work.

It is always a temptation when the dollars start to roll in to spend every waking moment working. It may seem prudent to work as much as you possibly can while going to school. You will find that excellence in schooling demands a lot more than the number of hours you spend in class. Too many returned missionaries have failed in school because they spent too much time working at their jobs. If you find that your work schedule is affecting your academics, you have a serious decision to make. It is going to require real dedication to postpone having the extra spending money in order to devote more time to schooling now. Most employers of university students will be sympathetic toward your school schedule. If they are not, be wise enough to seek other employment.

Be careful what kind of job you take during school. More often than you would believe, that job will become your life's career. If you have identified what career you are going into, try to get a job that will give you valuable experience in a related area. For example, if you are going into civil engineering, try getting a part-time job with a land surveying company or on the crew for the city engineer's department. Very often part-time employment becomes a full-time position once you have earned the degree.

Though a career-related part-time job is the ideal, you may have to work at whatever honest employment you can find in order to support yourself as you continue your education. If this is the case, look for a job where you can associate with other college students at work; look for work that fits around your class schedule; and if possible, try to find a job that allows you to keep the Sabbath day holy.

Whatever you decide to do for a temporary job, make certain that as you prepare for a career, you plan to be the very best you can be. You may be somewhat apprehensive about the stability of the economy or the availability of jobs in your chosen profession. Remember, there is always room at the top. If you are the best there is, there will be a position for you. Whether you are a plumber or a professor, if you are good at what you do, there will always be a demand for your skills. If you know how to work, you can always find work. With the drive and initiative you developed on your mission, you may very well find that going into business for yourself is the direction you want to go.

If the world seems like a scary place to you right now and

you are considering just waiting around until after the Second Coming, I would suggest you do just the opposite. In Matthew 24:46, the Savior lets us know what we ought to be doing: "Blessed is that servant, whom his lord when he cometh shall find so doing." This is not the day for the faint-hearted or the weak-kneed. We should use good common sense and be willing to take counsel from those who have gone before, but move ahead we must. Those who will be honored with millennial responsibility will be the doers, not the talkers.

If after following all the above counsel you still are struggling to find meaningful employment, try going through the ward employment specialist or LDS Employment Services. Sign up at a temporary service agency. Be aware, however, that the majority of the good jobs are not advertised. Let influential members of your ward and stake know that you are available. The more people who know you are looking for a job, the more likely you are to find a good job. Sometimes it really is who you know, rather than what you know, that makes the difference. Ask for Heavenly Father's help in finding a job, but then don't just sit there hoping something comes your way. We need to be "anxiously engaged in a good cause, and do many things of [our] own free will" (D&C 58:27) before we can expect the Lord to intervene for us.

Above all, do not be discouraged. The greatest blessings were all hidden in the second mile in the mission field; so it is with employment. The best jobs are always found on the last extra contact that is made when the other people have long since quit looking.

Intellectual Balancing Act

THERE ARE MANY REPORTS IN the media about how "Mormon intellectuals" are being singled out for persecution. The longer you are around them and the more you hear their arguments, the more you are convinced that they are neither "Mormon" nor "intellectual." That may sound rather harsh, so let me explain. When you hear the word *Catholic,* you probably imagine a person who holds to a certain set of beliefs. If that person deviates far from his belief system, you would call him a so-called Catholic, thus warning others that he calls himself Catholic but does not fall within the mainstream of Catholic belief. So it is with so-called Mormons who would seek refuge under the umbrella of Mormon theology but who differ significantly so as to be called into question because of their beliefs.

The dictionary would define "intellectuals" as those who "show high intelligence" in their ability to reason and understand truth (see *Webster's New World Dictionary*). When humans attempt to dictate how God is to officiate in his affairs with his children, they are hardly demonstrating "high intelligence."

As early as March 1914, President Joseph F. Smith warned of three dangers we would face in the latter days: "There are at least three dangers that threaten the Church within, and the authorities need to awaken to the fact that the people should be warned unceasingly against them. As I see these, they are flattery of prominent men in the world, false educational ideas, and sexual impurity" (*Gospel Doctrine* [Salt Lake City: Deseret Book Company, 1975], 312–13). It is impossible to live in the closing years of the twentieth century and not realize how prophetic President Smith's warnings were.

Having been involved in higher education during the decades of the sixties, seventies, eighties, and nineties, both as a student and as a teacher, I find it easy to see how a person can get caught up in how much mankind knows until we see how truly little we understand. A prominent child psychologist who during the sixties taught parents one method of child discipline later reversed himself and admitted that he had been mistaken. What about the generation of parents who relied upon his "expert advice" in rearing their children? No second chances for them. No "Oops, I guess I was wrong!" would undo the damage of the well-intended but misdirected advice of one "expert."

Your quest for facts and information today is no different. In the nineties we are hearing loud, blatant voices demanding changes in traditional gender roles, protection for those of an alternate sexual orientation, and the right to choose whether unborn children live or die. All of the intellectual dueling in the world will not replace the clear words from the Lord through his living prophets. Those who have ears tuned to the words of the prophets will avoid mistakes that bring devastating consequences.

Does the Church really repress free thought as the dissidents say it does? In all my academic studies, I have never been inhibited in my freedom of thought and expression.

What of all the media coverage suggesting Church persecution of "intellectuals"? Look at what is being said: "Give women the priesthood," for instance. In other words, "Dear God, you just don't understand what is best for your children. We here on earth with our unlimited understanding of the past and our clear vision of the future have determined that you are wrong and need to get into line!" It seems strange to call someone with that mentality "intellectual." Or perhaps another thought: "The Church needs to join the modern world and lift the stigma of sin from those who have chosen an 'alternate sexual orientation.'" That could be interpreted as saying, "Dear God, again you fail to understand. Although you created us, and although your sole objective is to get us back into the celestial kingdom, you need to loosen up on this issue. We know that anciently death was the prescribed punishment for homosexuality, but we're more enlightened now. We don't just want tolerance—we want full acceptance of homosexual couples. Perhaps you need to rethink the issues of marriage and family too."

My intent is not to mock those who so believe but to show how out of focus their arguments are when addressed to the Lawgiver. To dictate to God how he should act and what he should decide does not suggest a great deal of intellectualism to me.

Is it possible to get an education while being constantly bombarded with philosophies like these and still come away with your testimony intact? Yes, definitely. It is not until we as human beings come to think that we can replace God as the mastermind of the universe that our thinking commands center stage. We should have enough sense and humility to admit, as did the Prophet Joseph Smith, that "whatever God requires is right, no matter what it is, although we may not see the reason thereof till long after the events transpire." The Prophet continued, "He never will institute an ordinance or give a commandment to His people that is not calculated in its nature to promote that happiness which He has designed, and which will not end in the greatest amount of good and glory to those who become the recipients of his law and ordinances. Blessings offered, but rejected, are no longer blessings, but become like the talent hid in the earth by the wicked and slothful servant" (*Teachings of the Prophet Joseph Smith*, 256–57).

As you continue your schooling, keep your eye on the prophets. A daily reading from the pages of the book designated as "the most correct of any book on earth"—the Book of Mormon (see introduction, Book of Mormon)—will keep you from straying too far afield.

One spiritually fatal flaw of intellectuals is the compulsion to try to make the gospel fit or conform to the philosophies of men. If the gospel seems to be at variance with the most recent teachings of the scholars, intellectuals want to adjust the gospel. A more valid response would be to question the modern philosophy. Most of what I was taught as "truth" in the sixties has been reversed or discarded as "folklore" in the nineties. I would venture that such will be the case in the future. Any philosophy that contradicts the gospel will eventually be found to be in error.

There are many things we do not yet understand. In fact, the Lord explains that some things we just won't understand until he comes to usher in the Millennium. "In that day when the Lord shall come, he shall reveal all things—things which have passed, and hidden things which no man knew, things of the earth, by which it was made, and the purpose and the end thereof—things most precious, things that are above, and things that are beneath, things that are in the earth, and upon the earth, and in heaven" (D&C 101:32–34). It has become much easier in my older years to admit that I don't know the answers to all the questions. In fact, I am consoled to know that I don't even know all the questions. But as you learned on your mission, just because a nineteen-year-old or twenty-one-year-old missionary doesn't know the answer certainly does not mean there isn't an answer. So it is apparent that just because limited mankind does not know the answer to any given question, that certainly does not suggest that there isn't a God in heaven who knows the answers to all of the questions. Is there divine reason why the priesthood has not been given to women? Yes, and God knows the reason and it is correct.

There are so many areas of knowledge and understanding that will require our best effort that it seems ridiculous to spend our time and energy arguing with God about things that are not negotiable. Learning how to ask the right questions is a key to increased understanding. Learning to work within our God-imposed limits is learning not to be stifled but to be freed to spend all our energy in areas that will produce vital understanding. What a terrible loss to the Church and to mankind in general when those of high intellect choose to become adversaries to God. What wonderful revelations and understanding does God have in store for us when we redirect our efforts to discovering his will for us rather than dictating what his will toward us should be.

The Prophet Joseph Smith gave this solemn warning to the Church:

> O ye Twelve! and all Saints! profit by this important
> Key—that in all your trials, troubles, temptations,
> afflictions, bonds, imprisonments and death, see to it,

that you do not betray heaven; that you do not betray
Jesus Christ; that you do not betray the brethren; that
you do not betray the revelations of God, whether in
[the] Bible, Book of Mormon, or Doctrine and
Covenants, or any other that ever was or ever will be
given and revealed unto man in this world or that
which is to come. Yea, in all your kicking and flounder-
ings, see to it that you do not this thing, lest innocent
blood be found upon your skirts, and you go down to
hell. All other sins are not to be compared to sinning
against the Holy Ghost, and proving a traitor to the
brethren. (*Teachings of the Prophet Joseph Smith,* 156)

This is not a day for weak intellect or for people who do
not know how to think for themselves; it is a day to hold
tightly to the living prophets and to soar to unprecedented
heights both intellectually and spiritually.

18

FINDING THE RIGHT ONE

NEAR THE TOP OF THE LIST of concerns for every missionary about to return home is the concern over finding the "right one." Let's start by asking a vital question: "Is there a one and only one for me?" President Kimball said, "'Soulmates' are fiction and an illusion; and while every young man and young woman will seek with all diligence and prayerfulness to find a mate with whom life can be most compatible and beautiful, yet it is certain that almost any good man and any good woman can have happiness and a successful marriage if both are willing to pay the price" (*The Teachings of Spencer W. Kimball* [Salt Lake City: Bookcraft, 1982], 306).

Indeed, God, who knows the end from the beginning, knows exactly who we will marry. But since the Lord will probably not send an angel to tell us directly, we will be safest in taking President Kimball's approach. If we view every person of the opposite sex as a possible candidate for marriage, we will keep our eyes open and we won't miss the opportunity for a successful marriage when the right one does come along.

By far the better quest than trying to find the right one would be our never-ending quest to *be* the right one! There is a principle of the gospel that will help us in our search for a spouse. It is that "likes attract"! Note what the Lord said in

Doctrine and Covenants 88:40: "For intelligence cleaveth unto intelligence; wisdom receiveth wisdom; truth embraceth truth; virtue loveth virtue; light cleaveth unto light; mercy hath compassion on mercy and claimeth her own; justice continueth its course and claimeth its own; judgment goeth before the face of him who sitteth upon the throne and governeth and executeth all things."

If you want to attract a spiritual spouse, be a spiritual person yourself! If you want someone who is interested in scholarly pursuits, be interested in scholarly things yourself. The rest is easy.

Is it possible that someone with lesser spirituality or intellect or whatever will be attracted to you? Yes, but you probably won't be that interested in them, especially after you have gotten well acquainted with them! Is it also possible that you will be attracted to someone of greater spirituality or intellect than yourself? Yes, but again, don't be surprised if they do not show a sustained interest in you! When you find a person you are really attracted to, and they are attracted to you, when you see that you bring out the best in each other, when you want to excel and they do too, then you have a person whose name you should consider taking to the temple in humble prayer.

Too often the attitude among returned missionaries is "Oh, the Lord will provide!" That is a noble thought, but it demonstrates the same lack of understanding that Oliver Cowdery showed in the early days of the Church. The Lord reprimanded him by saying, "Behold, you have not understood; you have supposed that I would give it unto you [in your case today, tell you who your mate should be!], when you took no thought save it was to ask me. But, behold, I say unto you, that you must study it out in your mind [make your own preliminary decision!]; then you must ask me if it be right [you can't ask if you haven't decided!], and if it is right I will cause that your bosom shall burn within you; therefore, you shall feel that it is right. But if it be not right you shall have no such feelings, but you shall have a stupor of thought that shall cause you to forget the thing which is wrong" (D&C 9:7–9; bracketed notes added).

Finding an eternal companion is one of the most challenging and rewarding searches you will ever make. Don't be eager to shift the responsibility onto someone else. You—not Mom or Dad or even God—must live with that person for the rest of mortality and throughout eternity. It seems only right that you should make the choice of the person you will live with forever.

The soaring divorce rate worldwide has not altogether missed the Church. Keep this idea in mind: You marry who you date! If you don't think you'd like to marry a person, don't date him or her. You may say, "Oh, this is just a fun date." When you return from your mission, your focus needs to be different. Dates are still fun, but there is also a serious side to them. Before, you may have felt you could date anyone you wanted to because there was always that buffer, "I can't get serious because I'm going on a mission." We caution returning missionaries to date only those who are worthy to go to the temple. You can never guarantee where a relationship will lead. It may just be a casual date, but continued, close associations encourage feelings that are painful to extinguish once they are kindled. Dating someone with the idea of reactivating him or her sounds noble but is very dangerous. The apostle Paul gave this timely advice: "Be ye not unequally yoked together with unbelievers: for what fellowship hath righteousness with unrighteousness? and what communion hath light with darkness?" (2 Corinthians 6:14).

Take your relationship slowly. Eternity is a long time to build on a foundation of a couple of weeks. It is alarming to see how many returned missionaries meet, date, become engaged, and marry before the missionary has had a chance to assimilate. Relationships go more smoothly when there are not too many big surprises. Take your time and get acquainted before you get married! Just as you're wary of the high-pressure salesman who has to know "right now" or the deal is off, so, too, you should proceed slowly with the potential mate who has to know "right now" whether you will marry him or her. Love can and does wait. If a deal is a good deal today, it will be a good deal tomorrow. Avoid making hasty decisions.

Part of the fun of the courting process is to do enough things together that you see your potential mate in a wide variety of social situations. How do they act in Church or in spiritual situations? How do they handle various social situations that normally face couples? How do they interact with your family and friends? How do they react to stress? What are they like early in the morning? How do they act when they are exhausted? What is their reaction in a crisis or an emergency? How do they act on the basketball court or during a sporting event? These are all considerations that require time and experiences together to find the answers. To ask potential mates how they would act in a given situation is a poor substitute for observing the real experience.

Once you have found someone you are seriously considering as a mate, it would be wise to do a "celestial courtship" activity or two. By that I mean a date that goes from early morning to late night. Pick up your date at four or five o'clock in the morning. Go to the temple to participate in doing baptisms for the dead (remember that both of you need recommends in order to do this; if your date has not yet been through the temple, he or she will need to meet with the bishop and stake president in advance to obtain the necessary recommend). If both of you have been through the temple, go through an early-morning temple session together. Or drive somewhere scenic (perhaps a busy public campground or beach) where you can watch a sunrise together, cook breakfast over an open fire, and then hike, play tag, or sightsee until noon. Cook lunch over a fire or prepare lunch from ingredients you purchase together at a grocery store. At about 2:00 P.M. go home for one hour to get ready for the rest of the date. Meet again at 3:00 P.M. and tour a museum or art gallery. Eat at a nice restaurant. Go dancing or to a performance. At about midnight, return home. By that time the small talk is over, the facades are gone, and the real you is showing through. Because of the obvious dangers of being together too long, reserve this date for a time just before the final decision is made, and spend your day together in public places, not in solitude.

Now go back to your separate homes and evaluate the experience. Be honest. If you see no faults in your date, you aren't looking far enough. That doesn't mean you have to pick the other person apart; it just means that being aware of areas of potential conflict helps you make a more informed decision.

There is a game my future wife and I discovered by chance when we were dating that took some of the surprise out of marriage. We called it the "open-ended statement game." Because knowledge is power, we strongly suggest that you not play this game until you're sure you are getting married. It is simple to play. Taking turns, one person starts a statement, and the other must complete it honestly. During our courtship, we would drive from Logan to Salt Lake City (about a ninety-minute drive) and play the game all the way down and all the way back.

Some examples of these statements are the following: "My favorite color is . . ."; "The time of day I dislike most is . . ."; "My favorite food is . . ."; "The one food I dislike most is . . ."; "The ideal number of children in a family is . . ."; and "I think it's important to teach children to . . ." You get the idea. You will no doubt discover hundreds of statements for you and your partner to complete.

My wife and I had a great time playing that game before we were married. There was only one major surprise for her. She never found out what time I got up every morning. Because of work, school, and other responsibilities, I would get up about 4:00 A.M. She planned to be the ideal bride and get up before I did, cook breakfast, then wake me. On that first morning I got up at four. So much for her plan! We've laughed about that oversight for years. Playing this game, however, did minimize the number of surprises in our relationship. I hope you can see why you wouldn't use this technique with everyone you date. It would be tough to know more about someone else's spouse than he or she knows!

19

"Will You Marry Me?"

AFTER YOU HAVE DONE YOUR "homework" by getting to know a person, weighing the pros and cons of possible marriage to that person, deciding he or she is the right one, and taking your decision before the Lord for his confirmation, the next step is proposing marriage. If you are a man, your challenge is finding the right time, place, and way of proposing. If you are a woman, the challenge is to find an appropriate, memorable way of accepting his proposal.

From years of counseling young men and women who either have become or are about to become engaged, I'd like to suggest possible answers to several questions. You may ask, "Once I get a confirmation from the Lord, will I ever have any more doubts?" If you are typical, you will probably go through several seasons of questioning. There are at least two possible reasons for this. First, the decision you made may have been based on insufficient information. The doubts (or fears) you experience are not telling you that you have made the wrong decision but rather that in order to ensure future happiness in marriage, you need to continue gathering more information about the person you have chosen. Second, you may be experiencing the buffetings of the adversary, who is desperately trying to derail your plans for celestial marriage. You should note that the Lord does not use doubt and fear as means of communicating a negative answer to prayer. In fact, in Doctrine and Covenants 6:36 he states: "Look unto me in every thought; doubt not, fear not." Study section 9 of the Doctrine and Covenants. If you feel that "stupor of thought" the Lord describes in verse 9 of that section, you need to reevaluate your decision to marry. But if you have felt "your bosom . . . burn within you," you should feel good about your decision and move forward.

"Is it normal to question my readiness to marry and be successful?" you may ask. Again, if you are typical, you may experience self-doubt. After all, you have never traveled this path before. Many young couples want to know the end from the beginning. They ask, "What if five years down the road from now things don't work out?" I don't know of anyone who has a guarantee that life will be perfect five years from now. Because you have grown up in a world that emphasizes the controlling influence of the environment on the person, you may even wonder if there is some unseen puppeteer out there who, by manipulating certain factors, can cause you to either succeed or fail. The truth is that *you* create your own world. If you don't like something, the power is given you to change it. Although there are obvious limitations to your ability to change things, those limitations are not as many as most people suppose.

You may wonder, "Is it possible for me to get an affirmative answer from the Lord and for my proposed fiancé to get the opposite?" Yes. An affirmative answer from the Lord means that all factors considered, you could be happy and successful when married to that person. Do not try to impose your answer on your proposed mate. The last thing you would want is to "force" someone to marry you.

Marriage at best is a challenge. When one partner enters into it reluctantly, you are asking for serious, long-term problems.

It may be helpful to realize that instead of having given you a genuine "no" answer, your sweetheart may be "on hold." If the timing is not right for her to receive an answer, Heavenly Father may choose to give her no answer at all. When the timing is right, she will be ready to give either a positive or a negative answer. As you search the scriptures, see how often the Lord declares that he will do things "in mine own due time" (the phrase occurs thirty-four times in the modern-day scriptures).

"What if I ask and I am turned down?" you wonder. Life goes on. If the answer is a definite, unequivocal no, you'd better get on with life. Remember what you heard on your mission: "Your boyfriend or girlfriend may marry someone else while you are serving, but your future husband or wife will not!" The same is true in marriage: "The person you have proposed to may tell you no, but your true future husband or wife will not!" You will undoubtedly learn many lessons from such a painful rejection.

If you propose marriage and are turned down, end the relationship on friendly terms rather than making a childish scene. More than one couple have later decided that they really did love each other and were subsequently married. If you act immaturely or speak words that will leave lasting scars, the likelihood of a future reconciliation is greatly diminished. Now may not be the right time, but later on things may change.

Avoid using pressure to get the desired answer when you propose. On your mission you learned to be guided by the Spirit in knowing how and when to invite your beloved investigators to become members of the Church. Should you be any less sensitive in this eternally important decision?

Young women, if a proposal of marriage requires you to settle for less than you had hoped for, carefully consider your options. Eternity is a long time. Maybe everything will work out in the next life, but you have to make it successfully through this one first! You must seriously answer the question "Is a bad marriage better than no marriage at all?"

More likely than not, the young man who is asking for your hand in marriage is not the only one or the last one who will be available. Blissful, harmonious marriage can and will be heaven on earth. In contrast, look at some of the unhappy marriages around you.

If the man pursuing you has many of the desirable characteristics you want in a mate and you are willing to patiently work with him to help develop the rest, you may decide he really is what you are looking for. None of us will be welcomed into the celestial kingdom without having made some changes in our personalities and behavior, so don't expect to find an absolutely "perfect" person.

Even during the engagement period, you will want to continue the process of becoming more godly. Eager young people ideally looking toward marriage are more pliable and susceptible to change than people who have been married for many years who see no reason to make changes.

A young woman may also face the challenge of having received her confirmation from the Lord while the young man she hopes to marry is dragging his feet. In situations like this, remember that just as a young lady does not want to be pressured into marriage, neither should a young man feel pressured. Truly communicating your hopes, fears, dreams, and goals can help a young man realize that you are willing to work with him to make your marriage successful. He may mistakenly believe he has to solve all the problems alone.

Sometimes rejections to proposals come because of unrealistic expectations in possible future mates. It is still somewhat comical to see the number of frustrated young men who have been "inspired" to ask for the homecoming queen's hand in marriage. Not everyone can be the most popular guy or girl on campus. It is often very enlightening to look beyond the immediate physical trappings (over which we have limited control!) and look at the personality, spirituality, and sociability of the person you are interested in marrying.

Marriage should never be an extended period of entrapment. If your proposed mate is overly domineering or possessive before marriage, you may be surrendering your freedom and individuality if those problems are not addressed before the wedding.

We have looked at the possibility of rejection—which will more than likely never happen. If you have spent adequate time courting, the actual act of proposing may be a mere formality. Certainly the creativity you developed during high school and perfected during your mission can help you invent some unique but acceptable options for presenting the diamond. The main thing is to create a situation you will be proud to relate years from now when your grandchildren want to know how you proposed. What may seem clever or cute now may seem childish and immature when seen in the retrospective mirror of a few years. Use wisdom in your method of proposing. Sometimes a quiet, dignified way lends itself to your personality better than the flamboyant way. Remember, you make a statement about yourself in the way you propose. Say what you really mean and display who you really are. The ring may be the first tangible token of your eternal love. Make its presentation memorable.

20

ENGAGEMENT: LONG OR SHORT?

You have both made one of the biggest decisions of your life. From now on, everything will go smoothly, and life will be all sweetness and light—right? Wrong. You've probably read enough books, known enough engaged couples, and seen enough movies to know that people in love face challenges. Your engagement period is the time for facing challenges, getting acquainted with each other's families, and preparing in earnest for the greatest day of your life thus far—your wedding day. When you get engaged, you make a spiritual commitment. You are willing to give yourselves to each other at some time in the future. That is the commitment, although the actual ordinance will not take place until you kneel across the altar from each other in the temple.

Because of that commitment, the time of your engagement is a time of intense trial. You will be the most susceptible you have ever been to the temptations of Satan to become too involved physically. If you are wise, you will establish strict guidelines to keep yourselves clean and worthy to go to the temple. It is immature at best to believe that you can meet the adversary on his turf and win. Remember that he has had almost six thousand years of experience on many billions of people. He knows every trick in the book. The key is to stay off his turf.

Spending too much time alone together is asking for trouble. President Spencer W. Kimball gave stern warnings to those who want to make it to the temple clean:

> Too often, young people dismiss their petting with a shrug of their shoulders as a *little* indiscretion, while admitting that fornication is a base transgression. Too many of them are shocked, or feign to be, when told that what they have done in the name of petting was in reality fornication. The dividing line is a thin, blurry one. . . . The devil knows how to destroy our young girls and boys. He may not be able to tempt a person to murder or to commit adultery immediately, but he knows that if he can get a boy and a girl to sit in the car late enough after the dance, or to park long enough in the dark at the end of the lane, the best boy and the best girl will finally succumb and fall. He knows that all have a limit to their resistance. . . .
>
> Almost like twins, "petting"—and especially "heavy petting"—and fornication are alike. Also like twins, the one precedes the other, but most of the same characteristics are there. The same passions are aroused and, with but slight difference, similar body contacts are made. And from it are likely to come the same frustrations, sorrows, anguish, and remorse. (*The Teachings of Spencer W. Kimball*, 280–81)

How long should an engagement be, based on the above warning? Long enough to arrange for the details of the wedding and to get to know each other better but short enough to avoid problems. Some may be conducting their courtship from a distance, and if that is the case with you, you may think that because you are living in distant cities while going to school or working, the temptations will be less. Probably just the opposite is true. Infrequent dates tend to intensify passionate feelings that need to be controlled. If you find yourselves edging toward the inappropriate, seek the help of your bishop.

After my wife and I announced our engagement, our bishop called us in and warned us about the temptations we would face. He asked us to promise that we would call and ask for his permission before becoming physically involved with each other. I looked at my fiancée and she looked at me, and then we burst into laughter. At that point the bishop interrupted and said, "That is exactly what I wanted to happen. You see, when you become involved in sexual immorality, it happens a little at a time. Before you are aware, you have gone further than you anticipated and are really sorry, but it is too late. If you will promise to call me, you will break the cycle of intimacy before you get yourselves into difficulty, and you'll be okay!" We agreed and went on our way. As we left the bishop's office, he winked at us and said: "I'll probably never hear from you, but you'll make it to the temple clean." One night not long after that interview, we sat admiring the lights of the Logan Temple. As she sat snuggled against me with my arm around her, she looked up at me and said, "Do you think we ought to call the bishop?" We again laughed, and I took my arm from around her, bought her some ice cream, and took her home. It sounds silly, but we made it to the temple clean! I can envision times when you might use the same tactic. The chances of ever completing the call to the bishop are obviously remote, but breaking into a too-romantic moment together by considering whether you ought to "call the bishop" can help you control Satan.

Out of necessity you will probably be spending more time alone together than when you were casually dating. Plans need to be made, preparations need to be completed, and rules and procedures need to be established. These activities are not conveniently done in groups. Make sure that your integrity goes with you. When you are struggling to control your thoughts and you feel powerful sexual feelings, agree to stay apart. When you meet for your planning sessions, consider meeting in the library or some other public place where others are around you but you are also alone. Taking extra precautionary measures may seem unnecessary, but you will never look back with regret and wish that you had been a bit more careful.

Settling on a wedding date may seem like an item that doesn't need attention in a book. Just look far enough ahead to avoid any embarrassing delays or future problems. For example, if you plan to marry in December, make sure the temple is open during the time you are planning, as temples usually close briefly during this month. Many temples also close for cleaning for a couple of weeks during the summertime. Be wise enough to check in advance so that adjustments can be made if necessary. Consider your planned profession. If you plan to be a teacher, be aware that you will probably be teaching from September through May. If you plan to spend a "honeymoon" each year celebrating your anniversary, don't do it during the school year. I speak with the voice of experience. We got married late in September. For more than twenty-five years I have taught classes on our anniversary while my wife has been at home! We have just about decided to officially change our anniversary to the middle of the summer.

In today's world it is not uncommon to have the added

challenge of planning to include divorced parents or non-member parents in your wedding celebrations. The counsel of the Church has always been for young people to marry right the first time. The temple marriage of a son or daughter is a powerful incentive for increased activity for parents who have let their recommends lapse. Let the parents know far enough in advance that they can prepare to attend the temple with you. Under no circumstances should you consider trying to put parents before the Lord. Explain early that you plan to be married in the temple, and tell nonmember parents what that means. Multiple experiences with temple officiators who have spent time with nonmember parents have strengthened my testimony that being married in the temple is the only way to go even if nonmember parents can't attend. A special reception can be held in an adjacent ward or stake building, but a civil ceremony should never immediately precede or immediately follow a temple ceremony, except in countries where it is required by law. Check with your bishop. He will read you the section from the *General Handbook of Instructions* that explains the Church's policy in detail.

Most potential problems can be solved with calm, logical, timely consideration. When wedding preparation is rushed, feelings get hurt, people do not get informed or invited, and relationships are strained. Take extra care if you are enrolled in school the semester before the wedding. It is easy to let academic matters slide during your engagement. But then you may have to spend the rest of your college career trying to raise your grade point back to pre-engagement levels. It's better to take a lighter classload or set some strict guidelines for study so that you don't regret the time you spent preparing for marriage.

When we were courting, I remember someone saying, "The success of your marriage depends on how far beyond the honeymoon you have planned!" I think we had planned up to and including the honeymoon, so after hearing that comment we spent some time planning for the rest of our eternal life.

Amidst the thrill of the coming wedding, don't forget practical considerations. Plan for housing, transportation, utilities, food, tuition costs, clothing costs, insurance premiums, and emergencies. Soon enough the reality of life will be inescapable. If you have already considered the challenges, they won't be a big deal. If you get hit with the hard facts of life the day you get off your honeymoon, it can put a real strain on your new relationship.

Seek the counsel of those who seem to be handling life successfully—a favorite uncle or aunt, a trusted family friend, Mom and Dad, or someone in your ward or stake. But be careful not to let people make decisions for you that you will have to live with. Some of the dates that were the most fun and the most profitable were those when we seriously asked respected friends or relatives the how-to questions. Now is a great time to gather all the information you can to make those first few crucial months of marriage as enjoyable as possible.

A Time to Be Tested
in All Things

MARRIAGE IS A WONDERFUL thing. Unfortunately, too many people enter into it with unrealistic expectations. As with your mission, if you know what to expect, you will not be overwhelmed or surprised. If you have not been realistic, you are in for the shock of your life. Marriage poses the ultimate challenge. The following rather humorous account from Elder A. Theodore Tuttle of the Seventy has helped many couples put their problems into a more eternal perspective:

> After marriage in the temple, then what? I do not want to be misunderstood about this statement, but I want to say this: Temple marriage does not guarantee either success or happiness. It does not guarantee either success or happiness because these you must earn. The incident is told of a young couple married by President Stephen L Richards. After the ceremony, he said, "Well, now, young folks, you are at the end of your troubles!" So they went out happily into the world. After a few months of meeting some of the vicissitudes of life and having some problems they came back to see him and reported, "President Richards, we are having some

troubles. I thought you told us that we were at the *end* of our troubles."

He said, "I did, my dears. I just didn't tell you *which* end." (*Becoming Goodly Parents*, Brigham Young University Speeches of the Year [Provo, December 12, 1967], 7)

Nobody gets married with the idea of living in misery. Are we missing some gem of understanding that could put marital trials into a more eternal perspective?

Life seems to be like balancing on a tightrope. It is easy to fall off either side. In marriage, one of those tightropes is recognizing and solving problems. We can deny that problems exist until they become so overwhelming that the cumulative package is too big to handle and our marriage falls apart. On the other side of the rope are the couples who criticize every fault, every difference, and every mistake. Tender feelings are hurt, confidences are shattered, and love is replaced by resentment, hatred, and finally divorce. Is anyone living happily ever after? Sure they are, but not by living in a make-believe world. The world has such a poor track record that turning to worldly sources for advice on living happily ever after is not helpful. Where do we look for solutions that really work?

Watching couples solve normal day-to-day problems, some successfully and some not, has caused me to look at the gospel to see if answers exist. They do! They may not be simple but they do work. The following will not represent an exhaustive list, but it is a starting place to solving problems.

1. Put problems into proper perspective. While discussing the purpose of life with Abraham, the Lord explained that earth life was a time to "prove them herewith, to see if they will do all things whatsoever the Lord their God shall command them" (Abraham 3:25). Since the Lord is always true to his word, then we need to expect to be tried in all areas of life. Why should it be a shock to us that problems arise? It follows that it isn't the problems that are important but how we cope with them. It is our attitude about solving the problems that really counts. What a difference it would make if we would stop saying, "What is the matter with us? Why are we having all these problems? What are we doing wrong?" and start saying, "How are we going to solve this problem? What eternal principle are we to learn in passing this test? How grateful we are that Heavenly Father has so much confidence in us that he has allowed us to take a test of this magnitude at this time! How do we keep from disappointing him?" When viewed in a positive light, every problem becomes an opportunity to grow.

2. **Establish the ground rules.** Even before the wedding ceremony, a wise couple will do as you learned to do on your mission, sit down and establish how to deal with problems. If you didn't do it then, it isn't too late. Do it now.

Every young couple approaching marriage will come from two different backgrounds. How each of their parents did things will have a powerful impact on how they decide to handle problems. Some children will want to do things just like their parents because the parents were so successful. Some children will insist that they will never do things the way their parents did. The irony is that unless they establish their own way of dealing with problems, they will automatically default to the only way they know (their parents' way) when they experience similar situations. If you want to change your approach to disciplining children, spending money, solving personal differences, or a thousand other situations, establish the ground rules.

The Lord knows how important it is to establish a house. In the section of the Doctrine and Covenants entitled by the Prophet Joseph Smith "'the olive leaf. . . plucked from the Tree of Paradise, the Lord's message of peace to us'" (D&C 88, preface), the Lord instructs, "Organize yourselves; prepare every needful thing; and establish a house, even a house of prayer, a house of fasting, a house of faith, a house of learning, a house of glory, a house of order, a house of God" (v. 119). Isn't it interesting that the Prophet called this great revelation "the Lord's message of peace to us." If we haven't taken time to establish our house, then it shouldn't be surprising to us that we forfeit the promised blessing of peace.

How does one go about establishing the ground rules? In that same revelation the Lord gave some guidelines that could prove helpful. The first is timing. The Lord warns in verse 124 to "retire to thy bed early, that ye may not be weary." Usually, the times when we argue with our spouse or our brothers and sisters are when we are weary and not in control. Often feelings are hurt and relationships are strained because we insist on disobeying the Lord's counsel in this matter.

Verse 124 continues with a second guideline: "Arise early, that your . . . minds may be invigorated." We are much less likely to lose control after a good night's sleep. Many parents go to bed after painful, late-night confrontations with their teenagers, wishing that they had kept quiet until morning. Instead of helping the situation, the "let's get to the bottom of this" session turns into a fiasco. Likewise, many marriages are weakened because checkbooks must be balanced, perceived offenses must be talked through, and decisions must be made after reason and resistance have gone to bed.

A third suggestion is inferred from the confrontation

between Nephi and his older brothers after Laman's abortive attempt to obtain the brass plates. Laman and Lemuel were always focusing on the *problem*—even after being reprimanded by an angel. In stark contrast, Nephi faced the same seemingly impossible objective, but after analyzing the situation, he immediately turned his attention to possible *solutions*. It is important to focus on the problem long enough to define it. Then leave it alone and start working on solutions. Before long the air of depression (see 1 Nephi 3:14) turns into the spirit of optimism (see 1 Nephi 4:1–3).

A fourth suggestion comes also from the above story. Attack the problem and not the person. Immediately upon failing to obtain the plates by purchasing them (Nephi's proposed solution), Laman and Lemuel turned on their younger brothers to vent their frustration. It must have been a rather severe beating they were giving Sam and Nephi, because divine intervention was required to save their lives (see 1 Nephi 3:28–30). Very often in solving marital difficulties, we attack our partner rather than the problem. Since marriage encourages us to become no longer "twain" but to be "one flesh" (Matt. 19:5), to hurt our mate is equivalent to hurting ourselves—something only the seriously troubled do.

Instead of name calling and personal attacks, talk about how you feel when your partner does certain things or speaks in a certain way. When you focus on the way something makes you feel, a discussion can turn positive as you discover possible solutions: (1) your partner can change the behavior that makes you feel bad, or (2) you can alter your reaction to the behavior or situation. Maybe there isn't a right or wrong but rather a difference in personal preference.

A little understanding can defuse an explosive situation and cause reason to return.

A fifth suggestion is modeled for us by the Lord in his rebuke of Joseph Smith and the early Brethren for not building the Kirtland Temple (see D&C 95). This entire section of the Doctrine and Covenants is worthy of careful investigation, especially when it is applied to correcting children. The point is that the Lord doesn't leave the Brethren wondering what they have done to offend. He spells it out plainly so they cannot misunderstand. In verse 3 the Lord explains, "For ye have sinned against me a very grievous sin, in that . . ." Too often couples make the marriage-threatening mistake of saying, "I know what you are thinking." Since the Lord clearly stated that "there is none else save God that knowest thy thoughts and the intents of thy heart" (D&C 6:16), perhaps we would be wise to default to a very simple solution to the problem. If you want to know, ask! It seems so simple to just find out firsthand what a person is thinking or what he or she intended by a particular comment. This requires honesty, but if there isn't trust and honesty between marriage partners, immediate and more serious help is needed than can be given in a book. A simple "What are you thinking?" or "This is what I think I heard you say; is that what you intended?" will eliminate most misunderstandings.

3. **Look at the big picture.** When the Lord created the earth, he didn't tackle the project all at once. There was not only a well-planned, well-thought-out, well-organized "blueprint," but there was another divine example for us to follow. The Lord designated each completed phase of the whole project as "good" (see Moses 2:4, 10, 12, 18, 21, 25). When everything was completed God called it "very good" (see Moses 2:31). Often we fail to give credit for the things we do that are

good. We fail to recognize the progress we are making. We tend to focus on what we have left to do or where we failed. A quick analogy may help. If you took a test that had a hundred questions on it and you discovered that you had answered ninety-five out of one hundred correctly, how would you feel? Most of us would be pleased. Probably before putting the test away, we would locate the five we had missed and try to determine the correct answer. That is really the way we are in living the gospel and in living our marriage vows. We probably do 95 percent of what we covenanted to do. The adversary always wants us to focus on the 5 percent. In fact he tries to convince us that there isn't a 95 percent. How foolish! When a couple seriously considers all the things they had and still have in common that caused them to fall in love with each other in the first place, it is only reasonable to conclude that their 95 percent success is still intact. With optimistic enthusiasm we can then tackle the remaining 5 percent. Because we still have 5 percent to work on, would you say that we were "bad"? The Lord identified each completed phase of the earth's creation as "good" even before the Creation was completed. Can we afford to do less?

As a young boy I lived with some dear friends at Mapusaga, American Samoa. The only road that led to Pago Pago (the main city) was really a series of connected potholes. The buses that traveled the road were constantly broken down. Riding to town was a grueling experience, physically torturous. One day my friend and I climbed the Mapusaga Rainmaker, which towers fifteen hundred feet above the road. From atop the mountain, the road seemed to have direction and purpose. The potholes were unnoticeable. The jostling and lurching of the buses were not evident from our vantage point. I gained a new appreciation for the trials of life from that road. When viewed from a distance, things that seem difficult take on a whole new meaning. The same is true in marriage.

The graphics programs I use on the computer have a "zoom out" feature that enables the user to get a broader picture of the page on which he or she is working. We can apply the same principle to enhance our marriages. It's a good idea to set a time each week when, as a couple, we can "zoom out" and see our trials in a broader perspective. The Lord used that technique with the Prophet Joseph Smith, who had been inhumanely imprisoned for many months. A discouraged Joseph asked the Lord for a little insight. Two glorious revelations given as "answers to prayers" (D&C 121, 122) put all the persecutions, deprivations, imprisonments, and sufferings into eternal perspective: "Know thou, my son, that all these things shall give thee experience, and shall be for thy good" (D&C 122:7).

The pain and suffering of pregnancy and childbirth for both the prospective mother and prospective father would be unjustifiable unless considered in the larger perspective of the joy of holding a precious, new baby. Why would anyone go through that a second, third, or seventh time? We wouldn't unless we could "zoom out" and see that the joys greatly outweigh the pain. Marital challenges can be viewed the same way. Why do people go through all the trouble? When viewed through an eternal perspective, the pain and inconvenience seem insignificant. Paul tried to teach the ultimate worth of enduring problems by stating, "Eye hath not seen, nor ear heard, neither have entered into the heart of man, the things which God hath prepared for them that love him" (1 Corinthians 2:9).

4. Include the Lord in the solution. It is sad to watch

counselors of a worldly orientation advise people how to "get the most out of marriage." Divorce counselors are now realizing that divorce can actually cause more pain than staying together and solving the problems. Yet they still recommend that marriage be treated as a fifty-fifty deal, with each partner demanding his or her rights. How has the Lord suggested that we focus on marriage? In Matthew 10:39 the Savior gives the key to solving all our problems: "He that findeth his life shall lose it: and he that loseth his life for my sake shall find it." Perhaps this is the focal point of the chapter. When we take note of our problems but focus on helping others find happiness and overcome their challenges, a miracle happens. In the struggle to help others succeed, we turn to the Lord and ask him for help. And it often happens that as we are focusing our efforts on helping others, we find solutions to our own problems.

Perhaps another example will clarify the principle. Have you ever been in a cave and had your flashlight go out? I have, and it is dark. In fact, it is so dark that no matter how close you hold your hand to your face, you can't even see the outline of your hand. I remember fiddling with the flashlight to no avail. In frustration I focused the unseen, darkened flashlight into my face and struck it with my hand. The connection was made and on came the light. There was just one small problem. Now the light that was intended to lead me and others to the safety of the cave's mouth by illuminating the rocks, obstacles, and pitfalls was shining directly in my eyes. Gone was my night vision. In the brief second I looked directly into the light, I had complicated my assigned task (leading others to safety) by an action that I thought would help—but it didn't. It took some time before my vision was restored so that I could see clearly again.

Isn't that what happens when we dwell on our own problems? We become so bogged down that we lose hope of ever
solving the problem. Often, when faced with a challenging
mathematical problem, I would walk away from my desk for
awhile. When I returned, the solution became obvious. My
previous mind set had kept me from seeing all the options.

As the Lord tutored the prophet Joseph and others in the
proper use of the priesthood, he warned them of two potential pitfalls. Studying this scripture, we learn that we have
already qualified to be "called" to receive unlimited blessings.
If we fail to be "chosen," it will be because (1) our "hearts are
set so much upon the things of this world," or (2) we "aspire
to the honors of men." Because our focus is wrong, we fail to
learn this one vital lesson, "that the rights of the priesthood
are inseparably connected with the powers of heaven, and
that the powers of heaven cannot be controlled nor handled
only upon the principles of righteousness" (D&C 121:34–36).

If we are going to maintain power in our priesthood, it
can only be done as Christ did it. Unless we lead as he led,
love as he loved, and serve as he served, we cannot enjoy the
success that he enjoyed. Too often a husband wants to get his
own way by insisting that he holds the priesthood—so the
wife must obey! A careful reading of Doctrine and
Covenants 121:37–43 reveals that we are making a near-fatal
spiritual mistake by trying to use the priesthood to force anyone to do anything. Words like *persuasion, long-suffering,
gentleness, meekness, love unfeigned, kindness, pure knowledge,*
and *without guile* typify those Christlike qualities that make
marriage a bit of heaven on earth.

If marriage were nothing more than a "battle of the
sexes," I suppose couples could turn to worldly counselors
for a handbook on how to win the war. If marriage is to be

the final preparatory test for eternal life, then turn to the scriptures, the latter-day leaders, and prayer for guidance. I am comforted to know that "the Lord giveth no commandments unto the children of men, save he shall prepare a way for them that they may accomplish the thing which he commandeth them" (1 Nephi 3:7). He also commanded us to "live together in love" (D&C 42:45) and to "love one another . . . [and] learn to impart one to another as the gospel requires" (D&C 88:123). What an opportunity and a challenge, as husband and wife, to succeed in the greatest test of all time—the test to become "even as I am" (3 Nephi 27:27).

Intimacy in Marriage

IF YOU ARE EXPECTING A detailed how-to account of intimacy in marriage, you won't find it in this book. Your doctor can suggest books that explain the mechanics of sex. You may also want to ask your doctor for a marital guide book. They are available at a local pharmacy. In preparing for this book, I surveyed the available books on intimacy at a local bookstore. Few of the books I saw presented human intimacy in a way that was edifying or unifying. Most presented intimacy as an animalistic act between two people of the opposite sex, not as a unique, solidifying act between two eternal companions. (One exceptional discussion of sexual intimacy is Tim and Beverly LaHaye's book *The Act of Marriage: The Beauty of Sexual Love* [Grand Rapids, Mich.: Zondervan, 1976]. In this manual, the authors, who write from a Christian viewpoint, present detailed information while emphasizing the spiritual aspects of the marital relationship.)

If you turn to the telestial world for answers, you will find only telestial answers. If you want a celestial kind of intimacy, you must look to God and his mortal representatives.

Your understanding of the purpose of life has probably greatly changed in the past year and a half or two years as you have served a mission. Everything has much more significance. A mission should have given you experience in learning to recognize the Spirit and to use it in building, lifting, and blessing the lives of others.

In order to be consistent with the principles of eternal marriage, sexual relations in marriage should be built on spiritual principles. As you taught the gospel to others, you grew together, and you felt an intimate bonding of spirits as you saw people embrace the gospel.

Few people seem to realize it, but sharing spiritual experiences is the most intimate part of marriage. It will bond you to your mate eternally. Yes, the physical part of marriage is important and beautiful, but it is made infinitely more beautiful and more satisfying by the spiritual elements of your love for each other. Those spiritual feelings are based on principles you learned and practiced on your mission.

When you lose yourself in meeting and satisfying the needs of your spouse, you will find a beauty and passion in marriage that far exceeds anything the world can offer. Sexual experiences within the bonds of marriage can lift and strengthen you as a couple. In contrast, the worldly would teach you that your mate is a plaything to satisfy your lusts. This attitude is degrading rather than exalting.

Instead of accepting worldly teachings regarding sex, build your relationship on trust and mutual caring. Christ taught that when we reach out to serve and love others, it is the same as serving him. This is especially true in marriage. As you serve each other with all your heart, might, mind, and strength, you will feel a closeness and beauty in your marriage that will endure through the eternities. The world teaches you to find yourself by satisfying your own needs first. The Lord teaches you to lose yourself in the service of others, for only then will you find yourself. As you lose yourself in loving and caring for your eternal companion and seeing to his or her spiritual, emotional, and physical needs, you will find an intimate beauty that will grow deeper each day of your life. The Spirit will enhance every facet of your life, including the physical as well as the emotional part of your marriage.

When you have the guidance of the Spirit, you are more sensitive to your spouse's wants, needs, and desires. Your ability to communicate those needs to each other is enlarged when you live worthy of the Spirit. When you are able to control your passions before marriage, you build a relationship based on discipline rather than indulgence. Your Father in Heaven blessed you with passions and desires that draw you even closer to the person you love. These are good, godly gifts. When they are used within the bounds God has given, they will build, edify, and enhance self-esteem. When they are abused, they bring guilt, shame, and a lowering of self-esteem.

When my wife and I were married, President Glen Rex told us to always include our Heavenly Father in our marriage. Usually "two is company and three is a crowd," but this is different. "Counsel with the Lord in *all* thy doings, and he will direct thee for good" (Alma 37:37; emphasis added). This includes seeking a spirit of appropriate tenderness and mutual respect in matters of intimacy. You will have many questions about bringing children into your family, birth control, and what is "normal" and appropriate sex. Counsel with your bishop and with the Lord. I strongly urge you to spend a few dollars on an inexpensive booklet entitled *Sensible Sex* by Dr. Lindsay R. Curtis (n.p.: Lindsay R. Curtis, M.D., 1992). Doctor Curtis is a faithful LDS doctor with some good, sound, practical advice. In addition, as mentioned earlier, Tim and Beverly LaHaye's book *The Act of Marriage* can be most helpful for newlyweds.

While you were serving your mission, you probably felt awkward as you first approached people about the gospel. You may have been unsure of yourself because you were communicating with others in ways that were totally new. It's the same in marriage. Even though you love each other dearly, there will be many awkward times as you draw closer to your spouse spiritually, socially, emotionally, and physically. Marriage is a learning process.

You developed certain ways of handling those awkward moments on your mission. Some were productive, and some were not. Sometimes you may have become discouraged or angry with yourself or with companions. Sometimes you laughed at yourself and your weaknesses and dug in with new determination. Was it scary? Yes. Was it hard? Yes. Was it worth it. Yes!

There are a lot of firsts in the first year of marriage. There's a lot of awkwardness in attempting new things. There will be some frustrating times as you try to forge an eternal and lasting partnership.

The scriptures and the guidelines given by modern-day prophets should be the standard by which you judge all truth. Correct information helps you make choices in every aspect of your life. Make sure the information you receive from the world isn't in conflict with what the Spirit, the scriptures, and the Brethren tell you is right. The Lord has said he will tell you in your mind and your heart what is correct, so that you will not be deceived (see D&C 8:2–3).

The intimate part of marriage is sacred. Sexual powers come with a sacred trust from our Heavenly Father. These powers are used to create life and to draw man and woman into a oneness of body and spirit. These powers should be guarded carefully and only used within the guidelines the Lord has set. As you look around the world, think how many problems would not exist if the world would just listen to the directives our Heavenly Father has given on being morally clean. His commandments are given to bless us, not to inhibit our happiness. When we control our passions, we feel a sense of peace and well-being.

When we use our passions to bless our marriage rather than just to satisfy our physical wants, we build a unity and love and passion that the world can't duplicate because that feeling is enhanced by the Spirit and blessed by our Father in Heaven.

When you come together as husband and wife, having controlled your passions before marriage, you come with a greater trust for each another. You build confidence and self-esteem by controlling those sacred powers entrusted to you. The opposite is also true. When you misuse or abuse those powers before marriage, you lose trust and confidence in each other.

The Lord never would have commanded us to control our passions before marriage if he didn't believe we could. He has more faith in us than the world does and many times more than we have in ourselves. Parents and priesthood leaders can be a big help as we struggle to control our passions or to repent of past moral transgressions. Listen to the timely advice of trusted leaders.

There are many things in marriage that will require patience, humor, and understanding as you "become one flesh." Laugh together as you learn together. Probably in no other area of marriage is communication more useful than in learning about physical intimacy together. Be willing to openly and honestly express how you feel, what you like and don't like, what brings the Spirit, and what seems cheap and dirty.

Expect an adjustment period. It is not reasonable to believe that a lifetime of being warned against expressing your sexual feelings can be dismissed with a single ceremony in the temple. Be patient with each other. Time and experience will likely solve your problems.

Before marriage, it would be wise for both of you to have a complete physical examination. If there are physical problems, knowing about them can reduce tension after marriage as you both understand the limitations involved. The examination will also put your mind at ease concerning possible health-related problems. Sometimes a minor medical procedure is required to correct physiological difficulties that may otherwise impair sexual functioning. Usually that is not necessary. Like all other areas of marriage, the area of sexual intimacy is better if there are not so many surprises. I don't mean, however, that premarital sexual experience is in any way desirable. On the contrary, total innocence on your marriage night is probably the greatest compliment you can pay to your spouse.

Although physical intimacy is a very important part of married life, it (by itself) is not sufficient to hold your marriage together. Sharing intimate experiences spiritually, socially, and intellectually as well as physically makes you a well-rounded couple.

Be cautious about discussing your intimate experiences with others. Too often people compare notes. What a total betrayal of the confidence and purity of your spouse! Safeguard your intimate experiences with your eternal companion. Read the scriptures or listen to the modern prophets.

Since we are to use them as a pattern for our behavior, we should talk outside of marriage about as often as they do concerning intimate affairs. In case you haven't noticed—that is almost *never*. If you need counsel, talk to your bishop or family physician; but don't chat with friends and acquaintances about these intimate matters.

Like every other part of married life, the sexual aspect of marriage needs to be brought into proper focus. Sex isn't everything, but it is important, and it is divinely approved. This very power rightfully causes us to refer to God as our Father in Heaven. Even—or perhaps especially—in the area of physical intimacy, you will want to conduct yourselves in ways that allow you to have the Spirit as a constant companion.

23

CONFLICT RESOLUTION

IN A PRECEDING CHAPTER WE mentioned that tests and trials were an expected and normal part of marriage. Your attitude toward problems and your willingness to solve problems are of far greater importance than the problems you face. In the mission field you regularly held a problem-solving session with your companion. These "companionship inventories" were held to evaluate both the positive areas of your work together and the areas that needed attention. In marriage, since transfers are not desirable or anticipated, inventories become even more crucial. Many couples live together in an environment of increasing tension and distrust. Problems arise, but rather than addressing them, they choose to ignore them. However, because trials are actually necessary for our eventual exaltation, they will not disappear.

Before you are married, sit down and decide on a regular time to meet to resolve problems. As mentioned before, don't try to solve problems late at night or when one or both of you are mentally fatigued or angry. Set a time when you are fresh and the world looks manageable. In an interview with President David O. McKay and his wife of many years, Emma Rae, I learned one of the greatest lessons of my life. The person who was interviewing the McKays had apparently had a disagreement with his wife, and he was obviously irritated. The interview went something like this: Interviewer: "President McKay, you have what some would call a picture-perfect marriage. How often do you and Sister McKay fight?" President McKay: "Young man, we never fight!" In a voice that reflected disbelief, the interviewer asked: "Would you mind telling our audience how you keep from fighting?" President McKay turned to Sister McKay and said, "Emma, why don't you tell him?" She responded, "I will, David," then said, "We just decided that we won't get angry at the same time." By this time the interviewer had recovered somewhat, and he asked, "Well, what if you do get angry at the same time?" Sister McKay patted President McKay on the hand and said, "David, why don't you tell him?" President McKay said, "I will, Emma," and he then said: "If we ever get angry at the same time, we have agreed that I would go for a walk! And young man, I have spent a lot of nights out walking!"

Here was a key. A prophet of God telling me, a prospective husband, how to keep peace in the home. At that time I was majoring in psychology, and the theory of the day was that to walk away from an argument in marriage demonstrated a lack of true love. I had a choice to make: follow a living prophet or heed the philosophies of the day. The choice for me was easy—follow the prophet.

On several occasions I have found myself heading out the front door to get things into proper perspective. I don't know why, but when this happens it is always late at night, forty degrees below zero, and I have no coat. It only takes me a second to say to myself, "This is stupid. If I am mature enough to be married, surely I can be adult enough to reason this difference through." I return to find my beautiful wife also willing to talk through our differences.

132

If you are willing to make the commitment and the subsequent investment of willpower, you can go throughout your married life without arguing. Does that mean you will never disagree? Certainly not. You will likely disagree many times, but you will not attack each other—you will attack the problem.

Over a lifetime of observation and counseling, I've noticed that usually one partner is willing to ignore problems in an effort to keep peace and harmony and avoid confrontation. While it is true that couples should be willing to overlook minor differences, if the problems begin to fester and grow, they need to be resolved. Living together in the spirit of love requires a willingness to put aside pride and condemnation and a commitment to work together as a team to solve the problem.

Some of the factors that make for successful "companionship inventories" are seemingly insignificant but are very helpful to a smooth relationship. When you have your session, sit together on a sofa or at ninety-degree angles from each other at the table. Figuratively set the problem or the issue on the table in front of you. If you sit opposite each other and shoot at the issue, but miss, you hit your spouse! That is not good. We have found something therapeutic about going for a walk during the problem-solving session. The fact that we are moving in the same direction seems to get us on the same team. Whatever works best for you is fine, but if you find yourselves accusing each other or beginning to argue rather than discuss, check your positioning. And resolve to close your mouths just for a minute, until you regain control of what you are saying.

Have a set time for your sessions. Right after church on Sunday seems to be a good time for us. You are coming from a spiritual experience and are generally thinking in terms of the gospel. If another time encourages the spirit of cooperation, use it. Even if you don't have anything major to solve, hold the inventory anyway. That way, these problem-solving sessions don't become something to dread but something to look forward to.

Start with the positive. If you can't find anything that is going right in your relationship, you are not being honest. It might just be something minor, like "I really appreciate your willingness to put your dirty clothes in the hamper," or "It makes life much easier for me now that you make the bed every morning." Your inventories will probably consist of mostly positive things. It is not only okay but essential that you emphasize the positive and express your gratitude and appreciation.

During your inventory, select just two or three things to work on. If you identify a long list of needed corrections, your spouse may get the idea that things are actually worse than he or she thought. You have an eternity to work on your relationship. You come from different backgrounds; don't be surprised if the little things are the ones that become the real irritants. Almost always, the things that cause the tension are not the big issues but the little habits we have. Squeezing the toothpaste in the middle rather than at the end, deciding whether the toilet paper rolls over the top of the holder or out from the bottom, making the bed with the pillows under the bedspread or on the top, and closing the closet doors rather than leaving them open—all these are items mentioned by couples as areas of conflict. They sound pretty petty, but to the people involved these things were important.

After you have decided on the two or three items that you want to address, immediately go on to the "solution" part of the session. Once both of you understand fully what the problem is, start making a list of possible solutions. If you can only come up with one, you are not being very creative. For those who have just realized that the honeymoon is over, the first solution is usually that the other spouse change.

All of the skills you developed in the mission field—including negotiation, compromise, arbitration, and mediation—come into play at this time. Be willing to resolve concerns, view the problem from your spouse's perspective, and make concessions. When you come to a decision, make sure it is a mutual agreement and not just your spouse giving in to preserve peace. We resisted the concept of force in the pre-earth life, and we still resent and resist being forced down here on earth. If you're the husband, using your priesthood to "get your way" is one of the quickest and surest ways of losing power in your priesthood. Reread Doctrine and Covenants 121:34–42 and you will be impressed that force does not describe how the priesthood is to be used.

If you constantly remind yourselves that you are on the same team, these sessions will not degenerate into a power struggle or an argument. If necessary, stop during your companionship inventory and reaffirm that you are both on the same team. If one person gets defensive or argumentative, then consider postponing the session. Remember the admonition of the Savior to the Nephites:

> And there shall be no disputations among you, as there have hitherto been; neither shall there be disputations among you concerning the points of my doctrine, as there have hitherto been.
>
> For verily, verily I say unto you, he that hath the spirit of contention is not of me, but is of the devil, who

is the father of contention, and he stirreth up the hearts of men to contend with anger, one with another.

Behold, this is not my doctrine, to stir up the hearts of men with anger, one against another; but this is my doctrine, that such things should be done away. (3 Nephi 11:28–30)

As you mutually decide how to solve the problem, agree upon a time to check your progress, maybe during the next session. You may decide to periodically check up on the progress you make, but if you don't follow up, it is too easy to make empty promises without resolving the problem.

If all you do is accuse your spouse of things he or she is doing wrong, you are approaching the inventory in the wrong way. If you want to describe problems, try expressing them in terms of how they make you feel: for example, "When you leave the lid off the toothpaste it frustrates me because the glob comes out and toothpaste sprays all over the bathroom." As you describe your reaction, it alerts your spouse to something he or she may not have been aware of. A loving spouse will at least consider how his or her behavior affects you.

If you are not constantly working on being on the same team, it is easy to become adversaries. As you joke with each other, you may find that you are not entirely sure your spouse is joking. Unfortunately, this creates a vicious circle: Just in case she may be insulting you a little, you decide to throw in a barb. Then she isn't sure you are just kidding, so she sharpens her barb a little. Before long, feelings are hurt, the spirit of love is replaced by feelings of resentment, and what started out as fun has turned into a fiasco. Let your spouse know when your feelings are being hurt. You might say, "What you just said really hurt my feelings. Can you help me understand what you meant?" That puts the issue on the table and allows you both to stop and consider the direction of your verbal exchange. If you discover that you don't want that kind of relationship, it is easy to correct at that point. If you continue on to the end of a verbal duel, soon neither of you will be talking rationally enough to recover the ground you have lost.

In sports when you need a break to regroup and fine-tune your strategy, you call for a time-out. That is also a good practice in marriage. When you need a little room to calm down, put things into perspective, and get control of your attitude, call for a time-out. If you have agreed before you are married to honor that time-out sign, it will be a small issue to back off and consider what has caused the feelings. If you give the time-out sign, don't just forget what you called time-out for. If you need an hour or so to cool down, then that hour should be used to pray, meditate, study scriptures, list your feelings, and figure out how to solve the problem. If your spouse is doing the same thing, you will find that after the time-out period, the solution to the problem is obvious and fairly easy to implement.

It is doubtful that any serious-minded person believes that arguing, bickering, and fighting exist in the celestial kingdom. Sometime before we are welcome there, we must learn how to resolve our differences in a godly way. Isn't now as good a time as any?

24

DECISIONS, DECISIONS, DECISIONS!

WHY ARE THERE SO MANY decisions to make? It would be simple if there was always a clear-cut right or wrong answer. There isn't, and that's where growth is made as the two of you struggle to decide what course to take on significant issues. Some of the issues can admit compromise; others simply cannot.

How many children should there be in a family? That is a decision that must be made by you and your spouse after you have consulted with the Lord in prayer. If the wife wants eight children and the husband wants four, then six is not a compromise. It is too few for the wife and too many for the husband. Decisions like that need to be talked over before marriage. It is true that the two of you may change the decision after marriage, but it will be by mutual consent. My wife and I had decided before we were married to have a dozen children in our home. As the children started coming, we mutually decided to lower the number to six. Our rationale was that the other six would be the spouses of our children! The main point is that we both agreed. It was not a unilateral decision on her part or mine.

When should you start your family? No one can make

that decision for you, either. You may still be in school and question the advisability of having children now. You can, with confidence, approach the Lord for guidance on when to start your family. He knows your situation. If he inspires you to start now, he will also make a way for you to meet your obligations. Remember the conclusion of Nephi's inspiring declaration, "I will go and do the things which the Lord hath commanded, for I know that the Lord giveth no commandments unto the children of men, save he shall prepare a way for them that they may accomplish the thing which he commandeth them" (1 Nephi 3:7).

Should we buy furniture, a piano, a television, a microwave, or a thousand other things that everyone needs? Many times one spouse or the other buys on impulse and then worries that the other will be angry. No one can tell you whether a purchase is right or wrong. This is a decision that you need to work out between you. It will help if you reach an agreement, long before you make that first major purchase, that *neither of you* will purchase an item that costs more than $50 (or any other predetermined amount, depending on your budget) without first consulting the other. This will prevent unpleasant surprises—a spouse pulling into the driveway in a brand new car, an unexpected credit card bill for a thousand dollars' worth of clothing, and so on.

My wife and I agreed that we would take a couple of days to think over major purchases or investments before committing ourselves. As a newly married couple, be prepared for the rush of salespeople. Others will be eager to sell you photography packages, health club and spa memberships, expensive cookware, and other niceties. Some of those who sell things are very good at convincing you that you need the particular product they are selling, that you need it right now, and that if you don't purchase it immediately you'll regret it. If you have the money to buy every good deal that comes along, great. More than likely you will have to be selective in what you buy. It is essential that the two of you work out some standard phrasing if you are going to hold off overeager salesmen. Memorize some standard phrases like "I'm sorry, but I don't make purchases over the telephone"; "Thanks for letting us know about this great bargain, but we won't be able to say yes or no until we've had time to think it over"; or "Give us twenty-four hours to decide, all right?" If a salesperson says you need to make the purchase "now or never," I strongly advise caution. He or she may be desperate to make a sale, but that isn't your problem. Remind yourself that it's *your* money and that therefore only the two of you can decide how to spend it.

When we were first married, it seemed that everyone in our student ward was buying new furniture, new bedroom sets, new dining room sets, new everything. We couldn't quite figure out what we were doing wrong or why we were so poor at budgeting. Over the next few years, however, we became aware of how many of these families who had purchased all the new furniture were in serious financial trouble. That financial trouble had translated into serious marital strife in many families. Thinking of the challenges these friends faced, we decided our secondhand furniture looked really good.

No one can tell you whether a certain item is a need or a want. You must decide as husband and wife what standard of living suits your budget. The counsel of Church leaders is to get out of debt and stay out of debt. Of course, there are exceptions. You will probably not be able to pay cash for a house, car, major appliances, or maybe even your education. Be conservative in what you purchase so that becoming debt-free is possible.

Deciding on nonmaterial items like where to spend holidays is another challenge couples face. Balancing the social demands of both extended families is not easy. It is especially challenging if both families already have Thanksgiving and Christmas plans established and they conflict with each other. If you live a long way from either family, the decision of where to spend the holidays is easily made—of necessity you may have to stay home. It is more challenging if one family is insistent on keeping their schedule and the other is more timid. As long as you know the problem may exist, you can solve it before it becomes an issue of loyalty.

There will come a time in your married life when you decide you want to start your own holiday traditions. As your children get older, you can invite grandmas and grandpas to join you. That really solves a lot of problems for you, but it may create some problems with your brothers and sisters. Is there no end? Probably not—at least not until death. Just enjoy the challenges.

Decisions involving finances, problems, children, trips, educational opportunities, and so forth need to be considered. How much do you involve others? Who, besides each other, do you counsel with? How much of your personal lives do you share with others? There are no definite right or wrong answers.

Since marriage is a time of decisions, learn to make as many on your own as you can. There is nothing wrong with seeking advice from people you trust, but remember that you and your spouse will have to live with the consequences. Be careful about consulting with friends about your marital problems. They are not authorized to receive inspiration for you. If you cannot solve a problem, counsel with your bishop. If the problem goes beyond his level of expertise, he may refer you to a professional counselor. Your friends are in the process of going through the same challenges you are. Since they are still in the process, they are not sure that their solutions will eventually work either. To accept their advice may be to worsen your situation.

Your parents are only a resource. They may favor you over your spouse since you are their son or daughter. Wise parents will refrain from telling you what to do and will instead illustrate principles with stories. Unfortunately, most people are more than willing to solve all your problems for you. If you don't believe that, just watch the myriad talk shows on television; in front of a huge viewing audience, many individuals speak without knowledge about things that should be discussed only behind closed bedroom doors. Learn to turn to the one who really does know the answers. The Savior said, "Behold, and hearken, O ye elders of my church, saith the Lord your God, even Jesus Christ, your advocate, who knoweth the weakness of man and how to succor them who are tempted" (D&C 62:1). Later, the Savior again pleads with the people to look to him for help. "Behold and lo, mine eyes are upon you, and the heavens and the earth are in mine hands, and the riches of eternity are mine to give" (D&C 67:2). Still later he gives a wonderful promise:

> Verily, verily, I say unto you, ye are little children, and ye have not as yet understood how great blessings the Father hath in his own hands and prepared for you;
>
> And ye cannot bear all things now; nevertheless, be of good cheer, for I will lead you along. The kingdom is

yours and the blessings thereof are yours, and the riches of eternity are yours.

And he who receiveth all things with thankfulness shall be made glorious; and the things of this earth shall be added unto him, even an hundred fold, yea more. (D&C 78:17–19)

When you feel challenged beyond your abilities, do as you did in the mission field—go to your knees. Pray humbly for insight on how to succeed. If you are humble enough to ask every day for inspiration on how to live a celestial life, your Heavenly Father will not leave you alone to wander in this telestial world. Sometimes we complicate matters by involving so many other people in the decision that someone is going to be offended no matter what we decide. When the two of you gather all the facts that you can, make your decision, and take it to the Lord, often the clarity of the answers that come will fill your souls with joy.

As with missionary work, you will also discover that there is a time to make decisions and a time to wait. Before you went on your mission, you may have prayed mightily for an answer on whom to marry. You may have interpreted that warm, calm feeling as a confirmation that a certain person was the right one. What a shock when he or she ended up marrying someone else while you were gone! Had you been a bit more schooled in the way the Lord answers prayers, you may have discovered that he had just put you on "hold" because it was not yet time for you to make that decision. "In mine own due time" (see D&C 88:68) is a phrase I have come to appreciate more as the years pass. The Lord really is willing to lead us along if we are willing to exercise the patience necessary to receive his answers.

True joy comes when our agenda becomes one with the

Lord's agenda for us. Although we are the ones who are on trial here in mortality, the Lord has graciously offered to give us assistance when we ask him for help. Decisions are frustrating. Decisions are fun. Decisions are growth-producing. Righteous decisions help us progress toward the celestial kingdom. Have fun making all those decisions.

PLAN FOR THE FUTURE OR DEFAULT TO THE PAST

DO YOU WANT TO DISCIPLINE your children the way you were disciplined? Are your memories of holidays what you hope they will be for your children? Did your parents solve problems in a way that you want to duplicate in your marriage? These are questions without right or wrong answers, but they still need to be answered.

One young mother who sought my counsel was in tears and was very frustrated. She said something like, "I hated the way my mom disciplined us. I vowed that if I ever had children, I would never treat them like that! Now here I am with my four little children and I catch myself disciplining them the same way my mother did. What is wrong with me?" There wasn't anything wrong with her. She had just completed half of the formula for breaking an undesirable cycle. She had resolved what not to do.

The other half of the formula is not any more difficult, but unless you understand the process, you will likely not be successful in changing. The second part involves determining what you will do. This young mother and I had a lengthy discussion, and she left with some definite plans on how to handle frustrating situations. By deciding how to act in given situations, you too can enjoy the success that comes when you take control of your life.

You may be fortunate enough to have been raised in a home where generations of gospel living demonstrated correct principles which, when lived, have paid high dividends. Traditions are well established, procedures for coping with problems are firmly in place and are based on gospel principles, and success in marriage seems as easy as mimicking your parents. However, your parents grew up in a generation considerably different from yours. Although principles never change, your reaction to current problems will require ingenuity.

More typical are the young couples who have decided that now is a wonderful time to make a break with the old, unproductive ways and start establishing a life for themselves on a higher plane. How is it done? The same way you made changes on your mission. First, identify the things you want to change. Identify what in particular you do not like about what your parents have done. One easy example might be "We don't like the way our parents yelled at us." Now think of as many alternate methods as you can to eliminate the problem.

One enterprising couple confided that they would speak quietly to their children rather than yell. The more frustrated they were, the quieter they would speak. The children learned early that if Mom and Dad went quiet, they had better reevaluate their behavior. They used a swat on the hind pocket only to get the attention of the child. They had established a system of punishments that matched the violations. They had done a lot of homework, and although their system needed constant modification and refinement, it was working very well for them.

Different methods are required for different children. Not all children respond to the same kind of discipline.

You have probably heard of counting to ten before saying anything. That is just another tactic to help you be in control before you speak or act.

As in everything else, the Lord set the best example in how to discipline. As I have studied Doctrine and Covenants section 95, where the Lord disciplines Joseph Smith and the early brethren for not building the Kirtland Temple quickly enough, I have discovered six principles of godly discipline that have helped me in dealing with my own family.

The Lord begins by addressing "you whom I love," then adds, "and whom I love I also chasten." The first principle and controlling factor in discipline is the spirit in which it is given. If you can't discipline in love, don't discipline! This principle is so important that parents would do well to remind themselves of it every time they consider disciplining a child.

Several years ago, when two of our little boys were upstairs in the family room fighting, my wife came into the living room, where I was reading the newspaper, and asked if I would attend to the fight between the boys. I assured her that I would. I had already tried several times to go upstairs, but each time I felt anger; I knew I was not going in the spirit of love. I returned to my newspaper, not to read or even look at the words, but to pray and get the proper spirit so I could help the boys.

The second principle is also found in the first verse: "I also chasten that their sins may be forgiven." What is the purpose behind the discipline? Has someone dared to defy your authority? Are you disciplining because someone has dared to talk back to you? Or are you disciplining because you can see that unless corrected, your children's behavior will lead to serious problems later in life? Since every action has a consequence, part of our problem comes in our being able to know the consequences of our own and others' actions. Part of the discipline is to truly want to save your child from the negative consequences that inescapably follow violation of the Lord's directives.

The third principle can be inferred from the conclusion of that same first verse, which states that "with the chastisement I prepare a way for their deliverance in all things out of temptation." A deer that normally would flee from you will attack if cornered. Likewise, a child who normally will accept discipline may defiantly oppose you if cornered. Just as the Lord wisely prepared a way for the brethren he chastised to be delivered in all things out of temptations, wise parents will find a way for a child to be "delivered" out of his or her present inappropriate behavior without undue humiliation or disgrace. The problem is that a disgraced child feels completely cornered. There is no way out, no way to save face, no way to let off steam, and the child therefore reacts angrily.

In the example cited above about our two boys fighting, we eventually separated the boys and sent each to his room. Afterward, however, we recognized that all we had really accomplished was to stop the fighting. We both realized that the boys had not learned how to get along, that they did not, at that time, like each other, and that they did not have a greater respect for their parents based on our handling of the situation. We decided that next time, to avoid the frustration we had just experienced, I would handle the problem in a way we both agreed upon. She was to alert me and then retreat to the bedroom, lock the door, and turn up the stereo so she couldn't hear them fight.

The Lord seems to have a way of helping us learn lessons. It wasn't more than a day or two later that the same situation came up. According to our agreement, my wife told me the boys were fighting again, and then she retreated to the bedroom. Three or four times I started up the stairs trying to figure a way to stop the fighting, teach a lesson, and strengthen our relationship.

Finally, after a few tense minutes and a lot of prayer, I thought I had a solution. I went to the entry of the family room. Immediately there was silence. The boys already knew they were doing something wrong. They expected me to light into them. Instead I joined them on the floor.

We had assumed that they knew what the problem was—a bad assumption. Principle number four now came into play. In Doctrine and Covenants 95:3, the Lord was clear and specific in describing the errors the brethren had made: "For ye have sinned against me a very grievous sin, in that ye have . . ." The Lord took the time to describe the sin. I realized that it was important for a parent to do the same, so I sat there on the floor and explained that when the spirit of contention existed in a home, the Spirit of the Lord could not. I further explained that although they had the right to fight if they wanted to, they did not have the right to deprive everyone in the house of the Spirit.

With divine aid, I recognized a fifth principle and implemented it with the boys: I explained to them the desired behavior. The Lord did this when he taught the brethren of the Church: "Yea, verily I say unto you, I gave unto you a commandment that you should build a house, in the which house I design to endow those whom I have chosen with power from on high" (D&C 95:8). In a similar way, I tried to specifically teach the boys what we expected of them. Not leaving to chance that they understood how to act and why they are to get along, I taught them the principle of harmony in the home and the attendant rewards of such behavior. Things were going pretty well. As I spoke to them, I kept praying for continued assistance. After I had completed my teaching, I realized that there was one more step the Lord took. He helped them!

From verse 14 I identified principle number six: show them how it's done. The Lord taught the brethren by saying, "Therefore, let it be built after the manner which I shall show unto three of you." Now the boys and I did some fun role playing for a few minutes. I would pose a situation and have them role play the wrong way and the right way to act. We rehearsed about half a dozen situations, and their enthusiasm grew with each case. At the end I asked if they loved each other. They affirmed that they did. I suggested that a hug might cement the relationship. They readily complied. I asked if they still loved me. They both gave me a big hug as a demonstration of their love. I roughed up their hair and got up to leave. I got just to the entryway when my oldest son called after me, "Dad." He continued, "Thanks. That was really fun!" I knew then, in a way I had never realized before, the power that comes from doing things the Lord's way.

Wouldn't it be nice if I could report that the boys have never fought since? I can't. Wouldn't it be great if I could say that I have learned how to discipline the Lord's way in every situation? I can't. But every time I have successfully applied these six principles, I can testify of how wonderful everyone feels when discipline is administered the Lord's way.

Learning how to do things the Lord's way is a lifetime pursuit. You will not be perfect parents from the very start. There will be mistakes made, and you will alter and adjust your method of doing things. But when you continue to discover and apply the Lord's way, you will eventually find yourself making fewer mistakes in the most common areas of parenting. However, your understanding of other areas where you need divine assistance will increase. Will you ever perfect yourself in this life? Perhaps not, but the process leading to perfection is rewarding and fun.

Money Matters

Finances in marriage may not be the most important issue, but they seem to surface in most major disagreements. The amount of money a family has access to is not as relevant as how it is spent. As long as there is mutual agreement regarding most expenses and as long as there is enough money to go around, things go pretty smoothly. But when there is too much month left at the end of the money, tempers can flare and disrupt the Spirit in the home. How can these conflicts be avoided? Here are some simple, practical suggestions.

Using your mission experience as a model, make a budget. List every fixed expense. The first thing on the list should be tithes and offerings. Unless you are independently wealthy, you are going to need the help of the Lord in making ends meet. Don't offend him by robbing him (see Malachi 3:8–11). Rent and utilities must be paid monthly. See if you can get a record of the past year's gas and electricity bills. Telephone expenses can be controlled if you will agree to stay within a limit in your long-distance calling. Are you still paying for your car? Even if it is paid for, the law requires that you have basic insurance coverage. You must also calculate the taxes, licensing, gas, maintenance, and a fund for emergency repairs of a car. Eventually the car will have to be replaced. If you have saved for its replacement, the shock is not nearly so great as it would be with you coming home on foot because the car died without the possibility of resurrection.

For the first couple of years, you may be able to wear the clothes you brought into marriage. Eventually clothing costs must be figured into the budget. With marriage comes the responsibility of caring for your own health. Medical insurance can be very expensive but should not be ignored. Babies do come along and emergencies happen, and without some insurance you could be in real trouble.

Food budgets can fluctuate. However, it does require money to eat. You could set aside a certain amount monthly for food and then keep track of how much you actually spend; then cut back on luxury foods as needed, or adjust your food budget to match reality. Tuition, books, and other school expenses are other considerations. Because emergencies come, you are making a serious mistake if you don't set aside some money for emergencies. A savings account, no matter how small, should be set aside for Christmas, birthdays, vacations, and parties. Life can be pretty dull if you never have any diversions.

All this may sound overwhelming, but it doesn't have to be. There is a simple formula for adjusting a budget that has gotten out of control. Either increase your income or decrease your spending—or both! If we would learn to live within our means, finances would not cause so much marital friction.

As you plan your budget, if you decide that necessities will come before luxuries, you may find fewer reasons for disagreement. If you simply don't have enough money to meet your basic obligations, one or both of you must increase your hours of employment or get higher-paying jobs. Other alternatives include moving to a less expensive apartment, buying a less expensive car, or making do for now with what you have rather than making desirable but nonessential purchases.

You will probably find, like most of us who have gone before, that those lean years are some of the happiest of your lives. Struggling to establish yourselves financially can be a unifying experience. Sometimes your education must be postponed to replenish your financial reserves. You won't be the first one to take six years to earn a four-year degree! Being realistic and honest with your money can lay a firm financial foundation for the rest of your married life.

In light of all of this counsel, there is something I learned many years ago. This is directed specifically to the husbands. No matter how meager your budget, set aside a little money (twenty-five cents at a time if necessary!) so that your wife can have some "mad money"—money that she does not have to account for or that is not expected to be used to meet the necessities of the family. Very often the young wife is supporting the family while the husband completes schooling. Unless the husband is very sensitive, his bride can begin to slide into a hopeless depression because there doesn't seem to be a light at the end of the tunnel. It doesn't take much to cheer her up—maybe ten or twenty dollars. You take the kids for an evening and let her go shopping. Many of you men will be saying to yourself, "Just the thought of going shopping would make me depressed!" That may be true for you but not necessarily for your wife. If she isn't a "shop till you drop" kind of woman, she may want to visit a museum or an art show or just take a friend out for an evening. Your investment will pay higher dividends than you can imagine. She will come home a new woman. She may very well return home without having spent a dime, but just knowing that it is there for her if she wants to use it will be therapy enough.

A second suggestion that can enrich your life without destroying the budget is to make sure both spouses are growing together. If only one spouse is in school, the other spouse may get the feeling that life is passing her or him by while the other is learning at an accelerated rate. Community education classes are fun, educational, and very inexpensive. When we lived in North Carolina I was gone almost constantly with institute classes, institute activities, and speaking assignments. My wife was left at home with three little girls. When the mental fatigue of dealing with small children became apparent to me (which took much longer than it should have taken for me to notice!), we enrolled her in a community art class. By creatively swapping baby-sitting, she could attend class even when I was out of town. She blossomed in her self-esteem, felt rejuvenated, and enriched our home with her paintings. It was the best fifteen dollars a quarter we have ever spent.

Since that time we have always tried to find areas that she was interested in so that she could also continue to learn as I continued my education. Whatever investment you make in your spouse's education will bless you and your family forever.

Often the spouses' educational goals are very different from each other. With effort, you can use that diversity to increase your unity. My interest in art, music, productions, and cultural events has greatly increased because of my wife's understanding of these things. And her appreciation for athletics, science, outdoor activities, and academic pursuits has increased as she has participated with me. There isn't a right or wrong on what to like or dislike. The Lord has cautioned, however, that "if ye are not one ye are not mine" (D&C 38:27).

One often hears of wives who have supported their husbands through their professional training only to be served with divorce papers when the degree is attained. I can't help but believe that those painful divorces could have been avoided if both partners had worked harder at being on the same team. It is tragic when a Latter-day Saint man is so lacking in generosity that he allows his wife's interests to narrow at the same time his own interests and education are expanding. Sharing what your mate is learning and doing and sharing what you are learning keeps you on the same level. That doesn't mean your spouse has to learn everything you are learning to become a doctor. It does mean that he or she shares with you in those moments of pure joy when some difficult concept finally becomes clear. Your spouse can prompt you during your studying for exams. You can attend your spouse's recitals or displays. He or she can attend your annual Christmas parties. You can attend his or her favorite play. Making marriages work is hard work, but it's very enjoyable hard work.

In the rush of trying to make ends meet and schedules fit, don't forget to express your love for each other often. Be sincere when you say, "I love you." Love really is the lubricant that keeps the marriage running smoothly in spite of the disappointments, the debt, and the occasional friction that threatens the stability of your relationship. Common goals, agreed-upon sacrifices, mutual celebrations, shared disappointments, and togetherness keep the marriage solid amidst the crazy pace of those first crucial years of marriage. Enjoy the stress—you will only pass this way once!

PRIESTHOOD BLESSINGS

O N YOUR MISSION YOU SAW the priesthood at work all the time. Illnesses responded to priesthood commands, investigators' questions were answered, bad habits were broken, discouragement was overcome, and direction was given to those who asked for priesthood blessings. Why should it be any different in marriage?

If the priesthood is powerful enough to create worlds, move mountains, and calm stormy seas, that power can surely aid you in solving some of the problems you face in marriage. I am blessed to have a wife who has great faith in the priesthood. If she has a Relief Society lesson to give, has a problem related to one of the children, or is ill, she asks for a blessing. She has instilled that same faith in our children.

During the early months and years of marriage, there are so many firsts. It might seem a little awkward at first when you give your wife a blessing. After a few times it will seem like a natural thing to do. The priesthood is meant to bless people's lives. There isn't a possibility of depleting the power in the priesthood, so why be afraid of using it?

For you wives, asking for a priesthood blessing can be a way of waking your spiritually sleeping husband. Many years ago I was a young seminary instructor. We had been discussing the priesthood in class. A young girl came up afterward and asked me for a blessing. She explained that her dad, although he had been through the temple, was now a less-active member. She had a real problem and needed some divine help. I hoped it would work out when I suggested that she ask her dad for the blessing, and I reassured her that if he refused, I would be glad to give her the blessing. She left rather disappointed. That was on a Thursday. Friday she missed class—unheard of for her. Monday she missed class again. I was really concerned.

Tuesday she came running into class, threw her arms around my neck, and gave me a big hug. I am sure the class was wondering what was going on, so I asked her to explain what had happened. Through tears she told me that she had left class really disillusioned. I had taught a lesson on using the priesthood and then had refused to give her a blessing. She explained that she had skipped class Friday because she wasn't about to be taught by a hypocrite. Saturday she stewed over the situation but realized that I wouldn't give her the blessing until she had first asked her father.

She then told about trying to approach her dad several times but just couldn't muster up the courage. On Sunday she and her mom had gone to church, and when she returned home she decided to make the attempt. She described her dad as sitting in front of the television, unshaven, watching football with a beer can in his hand. She said she approached him and asked if she could talk to him for a minute. He told her to come back at halftime! She about chickened out, but she really needed a blessing so she waited. At halftime she confronted him: "Dad, I have a major test coming up on Tuesday that will determine whether I get a scholarship or not. Would you give me a priesthood bless-ing?" She said that he just looked at her, set down the beer can, and walked out of the room without saying a word! She was sure she had destroyed the fragile relationship that had existed between them for years. She didn't see him again the rest of the day nor the next day. She said she was so mad at me for putting her up to asking him that she sluffed class again Monday. Monday evening at dinner her dad was conspicuously absent. Partway through dinner, her dad came into the dining room. To her total surprise, he was clean-shaven and dressed in a suit and tie. He told his shocked wife and daughter that he had been fasting ever since the request for a blessing, and that if she still wanted it, he would be willing to try. Dinner was quickly forgotten. The blessing was given. Tearful embraces were exchanged, and a relationship was strengthened. She told the class that the blessing was not wordy or eloquent but very sincere. She thanked me for not giving her the blessing. Her father had promised to get his act together, and her testimony of the power of the priesthood was growing.

A few months later I met the father in a store. He came up and jokingly hit me on the shoulder. He told me what a shock it had been to him to have his daughter ask him for a blessing and how he had evaluated his actions. He explained that he had just received his renewed temple recommend and was planning to go back with his wife to the temple after a twenty-year absence. Then he gave me a hug and thanked me again for not giving his daughter the blessing.

Sometimes we men have a problem with ego. When we do the least little thing that isn't right, rather than face the music and repent, we just distance ourselves from those situations that act as painful reminders of what we ought to be. A good, goal-oriented wife and righteous children can make it difficult for us to stay off track very long.

There is no limit to the number of blessings that can be given. Before going to the hospital for the birth of each of our own children, we have shared a special closeness as I have given my wife a priesthood blessing. At the beginning of each school year, we set aside scripture reading for a day, and I give everyone in the family (including my wife) a special blessing. First dates, missions, college, trips, illnesses, tests, and times of extra frustration provide golden opportunities to draw near to the Lord with your family.

Establish early in your marriage a tradition of frequent priesthood use. For the husband, it is easy to bless others without ever considering receiving a blessing for yourself. Ask your home teachers to give you a blessing, or seek a blessing from your father or from your wife's father. It may scare them to begin with, but it will strengthen the bonds of love and family closeness among you. Appreciate also the priesthood counsel that is given to you and to other family members when you are set apart after being called to Church positions. The priesthood works for husbands and fathers just as it works for wives and children. Let the Lord bless you as you bless others and as you receive blessings from others.

28

When the Honeymoon Is Over

Do you remember times during your mission when you woke up and said to yourself, "I'm just not cut out to be a missionary"? That was the signal that homesickness had set in. But effort, perseverance, and hard work made you feel better. It is sort of that way in marriage. After a few months you may wake up and stare at the ceiling and ask yourself if you have made a mistake in marrying the person you did. That doesn't mean your marriage is on the rocks. It just means that the honeymoon is over. Those who believe that they can sustain the honeymoon forever are not being very realistic.

Let me explain: You *can* and *should* build your romance. Your love for each other will grow stronger every day. You will nurture that "honeymoon" feeling by continuing to court each other. But the fact is that school, work, financial concerns, and eventually rearing children will occupy much of your time from day to day, and you probably will not have the leisure to just bask in each other's constant presence for long. Practical matters will need your attention, and you will get on with the business of life.

When the honeymoon is over, you need to expand your relationship to include more than physical attraction. If your relationship is strong, your marriage will start to develop into a beautiful, full relationship. If it is based only on physical attraction, you may start to slide toward disappointment and eventual misery or divorce.

What do you do to strengthen your relationship? Do what you learned to do on your mission—keep communicating. You have probably noticed that spending a lot of time with each other over a number of months has given you a false sense of knowing what your spouse is thinking. Both fortunately and unfortunately, you are correct a lot of the time. It is fortunate because you can begin to anticipate what your spouse wants or needs before even being asked. You may begin to establish routines and schedules that help you know how to meet the needs of your mate before they even ask for help. That is good.

Unfortunately, unless we are careful we extend that "I know what you are thinking" idea too far. We start to assume that certain behaviors mean certain thought patterns. For example, when my wife and I were newlyweds, she came into the room where I was studying one evening and asked, "Why are you mad at me? Have I hurt your feelings?" I was totally dumbfounded. I wasn't mad at all but just quietly studying. I asked her why she thought I was mad and she explained, after some thought, that whenever her father was silent it was because he was mad. We quickly established a system that prevented either of us from assuming that we knew what the other one was thinking. The easiest solution is to ask! One timely "What are you thinking?" followed by an honest answer can eliminate a lot of hurt feelings.

As the demands of life increase, children come, and school or work becomes all-consuming, it is easy to grow apart. Perhaps the wife is at home bearing and rearing children while she serves in Church callings, and the husband is earning a living and also serving in the Church. Unless care is taken, you can become two strangers living under the same roof. Weekly date nights (even when you can't afford them!) help prevent a gap from forming.

As a young teacher I would come home exhausted from talking and interacting with students. My wife, on the other hand, had been home trying to carry on an intelligent conversation with a two-year-old and a four-year-old. She wanted to talk, and I wanted some quiet. When we realized the problem, it didn't take much ingenuity to solve it. We arranged with another young family in our ward to swap baby-sitting. We would watch their children for a few hours while they spent some time alone, and they would do the same for us. I found that talking to my sweetheart was a delightful interlude after a day of dealing with students. She seemed content to just be together alone sometimes. It was not so much the talk as it was the togetherness that really mattered.

Does the spark have to go out in marriage? No, you can stay in love and keep it growing as the years go by. Instead of trying to replace the physical attraction that you initially felt, continue to build on it. Add a cultural dimension by going to museums, plays, and productions. Broaden your circle of friends. During the courting period, you probably found yourself spending less and less time with your friends. During the early months of marriage, it was more exciting to picnic alone. Now you may want to expand your social circle to include friends, extended family, and those you have responsibility for (like your Sunday School class or Young Women class). Add an intellectual dimension. Keep learning and sharing. Read good books and talk about them. Visit the science museum or a historical site. Go to the planetarium or a dinosaur display. Engage in thought-provoking discussions with others who are still in school or who are specialists in a given area. Continue to increase your spiritual oneness. Regularly attend the temple, go to firesides, do family history research, go to family reunions and parties, plan trips to Church historical sites, visit Temple Square. Get into the habit of reading the scriptures every day as a couple and then as a family. Read conference addresses, Church magazines, and books by inspired authors. Give selfless service together.

Instead of feeling your marriage is collapsing around you, you will see that your love and respect for each other has grown immensely. I love to listen to older people talk about how much deeper their love is for each other now than it was when they were first married. That is definitely true. If you were to ask my wife and me whether we would go back to the honeymoon stage of our marriage if given the chance, the answer would be a quick and definite no. That was a fun time, but we do not want to lose what we have gained and learned together.

In addition to a weekly date, consider going on a yearly honeymoon without the kids. Grandparents, close friends, and others will usually be eager to help care for the kids. If you start from the very beginning of your marriage to plan these getaways, it will be easy to keep them going. If you wait until you've got enough money, or the kids are a little older, or there is a more convenient time, it may be years and years before you go anywhere together.

These outings need not be expensive or extended. A few days camping by a favorite lake, a couple of days in a friend's cabin, a quick trip to the beach, or a visit to a national park can do wonders for your marriage and for your enjoyment of your children when you return. Even one night away from the children will provide a pleasant break.

As your family gets a little older, go on some family retreats. Some of our most memorable moments have been when we have allowed the kids to plan for a few days at a cabin in the mountains. Each child is given a certain amount of money to plan for the meals and treats during the day. In addition to the informal time together, we also prepare an agenda for meetings during which we check our progress as a family in four vital areas: spiritual, social, intellectual, and physical growth. We spend time with each child doing what they would like to do. Wouldn't it be nice if the retreats were always perfect? Well, they are not. But the family loves these retreats, and when we come home, the children immediately start talking about when we can go again.

Right from the very beginning of your marriage, start some traditions. Some of them are silly and short-lived, but others will go on for generations. From the time I was very young, all of us kids in the family would gather at the foot of the stairs and sing Christmas carols until mom would wake up, light the tree, and give the signal so we could see what Santa Claus brought us. We have continued that tradition in our family. My children love it and will probably do the same thing when they get married. Another family tradition we have continued is having everyone tell something they are thankful for before beginning the Thanksgiving Day feast. At Christmas we all share one of our favorite memories from past Christmases. Hunting for Easter baskets, visiting ceme-teries on Memorial Day, setting off family fireworks—these and other traditions provide a welding link between genera-tions. You may adopt the traditions of your families, modify them to meet your needs, or start new ones.

Years ago my grandfather started the "Bott Board," which was just an old scrap of one-by-four-inch board about six and a half feet long. Every New Year's Day when we would visit my grandparents, he would measure each child's growth over the past year. The child's name and date were entered just above the line that marked his or her height. We have done the same thing in our family. When our boys reached that age when they didn't think they were growing fast enough, we dragged out the Bott Board to reassure them by noting their added height since the last measuring.

You will probably recall many traditions from both sides of the family. If you wait until later to start some traditions, you may look back with regret, because time passes all too quickly. If you are wise, you will plan ahead by making a long list of possible traditions, then working together to select a few that you want to start right now—or when the next holiday comes along.

When you first started reading this book, you may have thought you were just going to read about missions and the beginnings of marriage. Isn't life wonderful? It is full of surprises. Life taken as a continuous series of challenging events can be great. As you experienced and observed with your mission, you can have as rich or lean a married life as you want. If you wait for these things to just happen, you will likely look back with regret. Knowing how good marriage can be with just a little extra effort changes the focus from surviving to thriving. The Lord has given you the rare opportunity to "create your own world" by starting your family. If you want a rich, colorful world, create one for yourself. The choice is yours.

Spend some time with older people and ask them what they did to create memories, what they wish they had done, what they are glad they did, and what they would do if they had it all to do over again. You will hear a lot of advice, some good, some bad. But at least you'll have something to choose from. Sometimes when I hear a really good idea, I think, Wow! I wish we had known that years ago when our kids were young.

Life can be full and rich. There will always be a new twist to make life more exciting. When you are dedicated to living life to its fullest, you can find ways to make even the challenges more fun. Follow the prophets and Church leaders and you will have ample time to enjoy the good life.

Life is not a destination; it is a journey. Learn to enjoy the journey. If you are not really enjoying life, what are you doing wrong? Everything will not always go perfectly. But making lemonade out of lemons is much more fun than treating citric acid burns. Is married life heaven on earth? It can be! A wise man once gave the following reply to a question about how difficult it is to make it to the celestial kingdom: "It is easy if you work at it hard and hard if you work at it easy." The same applies to a blissful married life.

29

PRIORITIES

WOULDN'T IT BE GREAT IF AN angel came down and gave us a list of what is really important in God's eyes? Well, as a matter of fact, there is such a list. If you are interested in knowing the order in which your earthly stewardship is to be accounted to the Savior, the following statement given by President David O. McKay in June 1965 to the employees of the Physical Facilities Department of the Church will be priceless. While explaining to them the importance of the work they were engaged in, he paused and told them the following:

> Let me assure you, brethren, that someday you will have a personal priesthood interview with the Savior Himself. If you are interested, I will tell you the order in which He will ask you to account for your earthly responsibilities.
>
> First, He will request an accountability report about your relationship with your wife. Have you actively been engaged in making her happy and ensuring that her needs have been met as an individual?
>
> Second, He will want an accountability report about each of your children individually. He will not attempt to have this for simply a family stewardship but will

request information about your relationship to each
and every child. Third, He will want to know what you
personally have done with the talents you were given in
the preexistence.

Fourth, He will want a summary of your activity in
your Church assignments. He will not be necessarily
interested in what assignments you have had, for in His
eyes the home teacher and a mission president are
probably equals, but He will request a summary of how
you have been of service to your fellowmen in your
Church assignments.

Fifth, He will have no interest in how you earned
your living, but [instead in whether] you were honest
in all your dealings.

Sixth, He will ask for an accountability on what you
have done to contribute in a positive manner to your
community, state, country and the world. (From notes
of Fred A. Baker, Managing Director, Department of
Physical Facilities)

If you use that prophetic outline as a guide, it should be
fairly easy to keep your priorities straight. When we put
things of secondary importance in primary positions, our
whole life seems to be in a state of turmoil. It is a real temptation during the early days of marriage to become a worka-
holic in an attempt to acquire all that your parents have
accumulated over a lifetime. It is an even greater temptation
to rationalize that school has to come first for the next few
years! President McKay was famous for his observation, "No
other success can compensate for failure in the home" (J. E.
McCulloch, as quoted by David O. McKay, in Conference
Report, April 1935, p. 116; April 1964, p. 5). The Savior asked
a very sobering question: "For what is a man profited, if he

shall gain the whole world, and lose his own soul? or what shall a man give in exchange for his soul?" (Matthew 16:26).

Almost all of us who are advancing in years look back with some regret at how we misplaced priorities in the early days of our marriage. The scriptures were there and the prophets were speaking, but we may not have been listening as intently as we should.

Review often President McKay's advice. Before work, school, recreation, or children come the needs of your mate. Doctrine and Covenants 42:22 clarifies the importance of the marriage relationship: "Thou shalt love thy wife with all thy heart, and shalt cleave unto her and none else." President Spencer W. Kimball commented on that passage of scripture as follows: "The words *none else* eliminate everyone and everything. The spouse then becomes preeminent in the life of the husband or wife and neither social life nor occupational life nor political life nor any other interest nor person nor thing shall ever take precedence over the companion spouse. We sometimes find women who absorb and hover over the children at the expense of the husband, sometimes even estranging them from him. This is in direct violation of the command: *None else*" (*The Miracle of Forgiveness,* [Salt Lake City: Bookcraft, 1969], 250–51).

Take time to be with and strengthen your children. Rearing children can be frustrating. They will not always be totally obedient. In spite of your best efforts, some may develop bad attitudes or may even be rebellious. Their challenging behavior may have nothing to do with your failure. Children have agency. It is intriguing to note that in the parable of the prodigal son (see Luke 15:11–32), the father does not condemn himself or hold himself responsible for the behavior of the younger son—even though he provided the means for his son to enjoy the party life. If we follow the inspired counsel of our leaders, very few of our children will permanently leave the fold although some may stray for a while.

The third area of accountability mentioned by President McKay is your accountability for developing those talents and gifts given to you. Identifying those talents and using them to bless others is part of the challenge of life. If your world is not what you want it to be, don't wait for someone to change it; change it yourself. Elder Richard L. Evans of the Quorum of the Twelve gave some solid advice in the April 1961 general conference: "Now, as to a willingness to work: Nothing ever does itself. Nothing ever memorizes itself. Nothing ever accomplishes itself—without the requisite effort. Carlyle said, 'Men do less than they ought, unless they do all that they can.' It is not enough just to try; we have to succeed. The Lord expects us to see things through" (in Conference Report, April 1961, 75–76).

President McKay's fourth point is vital to happiness in the Church. Many people aspire to be bishops, Relief Society presidents, stake presidents, or General Authorities because of the visibility of men and women in those positions. It is how we serve, not where, that makes the difference. Countless unnamed Latter-day Saints labor without recognition to make the kingdom of God on earth roll forward in preparation for the arrival of the kingdom of heaven. Worry more about service and less about who gets the credit, and you will have a full, rich life.

The fifth point is integrity in the workplace. Giving a day's work for a day's pay is a disappearing philosophy. Happy indeed is the returned missionary who finds joy in his or her work. Work is honorable and divinely approved. Our first mortal father, Adam, was informed that the earth had been "cursed . . . for thy sake" (Genesis 3:17). Trying to get into a financial position where you don't have to work is in direct opposition to the divine plan. Being financially successful is not bad or undesirable if your desire is to promote the cause of Zion in these last days. Money does not canker a person's soul. It is the love of money that is the root of all evil (see 1 Timothy 6:10). Making the most of your time in mortality is not only desirable but commanded: "Thou shalt not idle away thy time, neither shalt thou bury thy talent that it may not be known" (D&C 60:13). It seems apparent that if we worked at or near our capacity, using all of our God-given talents, we would have just enough time to complete that which we were assigned to do in mortality. The Lord taught us that truth by saying, "For there is a time appointed for every man, according as his works shall be" (D&C 121:25). Part of the regret that we may yet suffer may come when we are shown what we could have accomplished if we had wisely used our time.

The final area of accountability will be the contribution we have made outside our home. It is easy to look with disgust at the world, to shake our heads in disbelief, and to go on about our own family's business. Recent tragedies and disasters reported in the news should help us realize that we cannot afford to ignore the plight of the world.

We as Latter-day Saints, more than any other people, have the solutions to the world's problems. They have been revealed by the Lord. As we use our knowledge of the gospel and the warnings from Latter-day prophets, we can give light to a darkening world. The Savior commanded us, "Therefore, hold up your light that it may shine unto the world. Behold I am the light which ye shall hold up—that which ye have seen me do" (3 Nephi 18:24). Changing the world may seem like an overwhelming task. The Savior knew what we would be facing. He consoled us by saying, "Wherefore, be not weary in well-doing, for ye are laying the foundation of a great work. And out of small things proceedeth that which is great" (D&C 64:33). Do your part and you will be able to report your stewardship without fear or regret.

30

FOREVER MORE

THOUSANDS OF BOOKS HAVE been written about how to have a successful marriage. Attitude seems to be the most important factor. Whether you think you can or you can't be successful, you are right! As you marry in the temple you will complete, as far as ordinances are concerned, all that is necessary for you to gain exaltation.

Does that mean you have arrived? Certainly not! You have only entered through the gate that leads to the path to the celestial kingdom. Doctrine and Covenants 132:7 outlines in three short phrases what will take you and your spouse a lifetime to accomplish: "All covenants . . . that are not made and entered into and sealed by the Holy Spirit of promise . . . are of no efficacy, virtue, or force . . . after the resurrection from the dead." How do you "make" the covenant of marriage? That is what you do when you kneel across the altar from each other in the temple! How do you "enter into" the covenant of marriage? That requires a lifetime. It means to live by every promise that you have made to each other. It means to treat each other like the king and queen you are destined to become. It means meeting and overcoming together all the problems that Heavenly Father has seen fit to allow you to tackle in the test called mortality. It means becoming one. It means identifying and overcoming weaknesses. It means being humble enough to accept whatever the Lord deems necessary for us to experience. It means learning how to honor the priesthood by serving our family and serving in the Church. It means following the living prophets' counsel and the counsel in the scriptures. It means taking advantage of every opportunity to further the kingdom of God. It means magnifying our own callings and letting others magnify theirs. It means teaching and leading and loving children so that we may learn how to become eternal parents. It means returning frequently to the temple to renew and review the covenants we have made. It means living with one eye constantly trained on eternity while making the most of mortality. It means overcoming the temptations Satan constantly throws our way. It means subduing and gaining dominion over our world in preparation for creating our own world. It means not resting until we have passed every test of life and have together made our calling and election sure.

Does that sound like something you will accomplish during the first year of marriage? During the first decade? Perhaps not even during the first half century, or maybe not until long after you have passed through the veil into the life after death.

It is a little scary to look at the number of people who are temporarily failing the exam. We see many who have lost the vision of what life is all about and have forgotten what is in store for those who succeed. Some only see how rapidly the world is deteriorating and worry about how their children will ever be able to cope. If the Lord did not think it was possible for us to succeed under such trying circumstances, he would not have put us here now.

When we stand on the other side of the veil and have

perfect memory of our premortal life, we will see that we anxiously looked forward to mortality. The Lord in his infinite wisdom chose us to be here at this time.

Although the challenge is almost overwhelming, President Ezra Taft Benson put that challenge into proper perspective:

> For nearly six thousand years, God has held you in reserve to make your appearance in the final days before the Second Coming of the Lord. . . . While our generation will be comparable in wickedness to the days of Noah, when the Lord cleansed the earth by flood, there is a major difference this time. It is that God has saved for the final inning some of his strongest children, who will help bear off the Kingdom triumphantly. And that is where you come in, for you are the generation that must be prepared to meet your God.
>
> All through the ages the prophets have looked down through the corridors of time to our day. Billions of the deceased and those yet to be born have their eyes on us. Make no mistake about it—you are a marked generation. There has never been more expected of the faithful in such a short period of time as there is of us. Never before on the face of this earth have the forces of evil and the forces of good been as well organized. Now is the great day of the devil's power, with the greatest mass murderers of all time living among us. But now is also the great day of the Lord's power, with the greatest number ever of priesthood holders on the earth. And the showdown is fast approaching. ("In His Steps," *Speeches of the Year*, 1979 [Provo: Brigham Young University Press, 1980], p. 59)

Your full-time proselyting mission is complete. You have successfully completed the most difficult assignment that God has laid upon your shoulders—up to this point in time. You might say you've honorably completed the pre-game warmup. Now is the time to join the spiritually mature members of the Church upon whose shoulders the Lord has placed the responsibility of preparing the Church and the world for his second coming.

This is not the day for the weak and fainthearted. It is not a day for spiritual sabbaticals or lukewarm effort. Between now and the Second Coming, we will face problems that we have never encountered before and opposition that is greater than ever before. There are meetings to attend—regular ward, stake, and general Church meetings and special meetings at Adam-ondi-Ahman. There are seats of leadership to fill, additional missions to serve, sacrifices to be made.

In one hundred years the world will scarcely resemble what we now see. Whether we have kept pace with the Church or not is up to us. Whether you choose to keep pace or not, the test will be over for you and me before another hundred years pass. The rest of eternity will be spent enjoying or regretting the choices we have made.

Thousands of years ago we joined the choirs "when the morning stars sang together, and all the sons of God shouted for joy" (Job 38:7). Assignments were given and responsibilities accepted. Surely we must have been impatiently waiting for our turn to serve. You prepared with honor during those long ages of pre-earth life and for the first few years of your mortal life. You served with honor for eighteen months or two years in your mission area. Now you are returning with honor from your full-time mission in order to continue an even greater mission in life—including marrying and rearing children. Someday, will you return with honor to the anxious, waiting arms of your Heavenly Father?

Live one day at a time. Live each day so that you can look back without regret. What a thrill to know that God has enough confidence in you to allow you to be who you are, to be on the first string during the final minutes of the fourth quarter of the greatest game ever played. Don't shortchange yourself by giving less than your best. Don't disappoint the Lord by losing sight of who you are and what you are sent to do.

There is a God in heaven. He is at the helm. Nothing that is happening or will happen is a surprise to him or beyond his power to control. He is willing to continue to communicate directly with you as you humbly and willingly serve him. May we join with countless others on both sides of the veil in saying to you, "Welcome home, elder. Welcome home, sister." Eventually the Lord will personally greet you. His words of welcome are recorded for you to read: "Well done, thou good and faithful servant: thou hast been faithful over a few things, I will make thee ruler over many things: enter thou into the joy of thy lord" (Matthew 25:21). The Lord wants you to return with honor.

31

FUN DATES AND GROUP
ACTIVITIES

HERE ARE A FEW IDEAS FOR inexpensive, fun dates. If you browse through a bookstore, you will find that several books have been written on the subject, providing a wealth of ideas and possibilities.

> Anonymous service project
> Antique hunting
> Archery
> Auction
> Baby-sitting
> Backwards party
> Badminton
> Barbecue
> Barn party
> Baseball game (play or watch)
> Baseball in the rain
> Basketball (play or watch)
> Beach party
> Bike riding
> Bingo
> Bird watching
> Boating

Body surfing
Bottle-feeding calves
Bow hunting
Bowling
Breakfast
Bridge building (use toothpicks or popsicle sticks)
Bubblegum party
Bubble-blowing contest
Bug collecting
Building a snowman
Building stilts and using them
Bus ride around town
Cake baking
Cake decorating
Candlelight dinner at McDonald's
Candlelight dinner in a pickup truck
Candy apples
Candy making
Canoeing
Carnival
Caroling
Cattle drive
Cattle show
Charades
Checkers
Church activities
Church meetings
Circus
Cleanup projects
Climbing trees
Collect a meal for charity
Coloring in coloring books

Come-as-you-are party
Concerts
Conducting a poll
Cookie baking
Cooking dinner together
Cops and Robbers game
Crazy dinner
Crochet (teach each other)
Dancing
Decorating newlyweds' car
Demolition derby
Developing pictures
Dictionary game
Diving
Double-date with parents
Drag races
Dyeing Easter eggs (anytime)
Early-morning breakfast
Eating (at home, drive-in, restaurant)
Exploring cave or new sites
Fair (county or state)
Fifty-cent date
Fishing
Flour-bag fight
Fluorescent ball in dark room
Flying kites
Flying paper airplanes
Fly tying
Fondue party
Football game (play or watch)
Football in the dark
Football in the snow

Formal dinner in wilderness
Frisbee throwing
Glacier sliding
Go-carts (make and race)
Golf
Gravel-pit tag
Greased pig chase
Grocery shopping
Gutter boating (cucumber boats)
Hair styling
Halloweening
Handball
Hayride
Hide and Seek
Hiking
Hill climbing
Hoagie sandwiches (make and eat)
Hockey (watch or play)
Home decorating (rearranging)
Hopscotch
Horseback riding
Hot air balloon
Hunting (all kinds)
Hunting four-leaf clovers
Ice cream (make and eat)
Ice skating
Icing (sliding down a hill on a block of ice)
Jacks
Jeep riding
Jet skiing
Jogging (day and night)
Kick the Can

"Kidnap" date (with permission)
Kids' games
King of Bunker's Hill
Leaf collecting
Light show (homemade)
Making a gingerbread house
Making a movie
Marbles
Milking cows
Miniature golf
Mission Impossible Game
Model cars, planes, etc.
Motorcycle races
Motorcycle riding
Movie (drive-in, theater)
Mud fights
Murder in the Dark (game)
Museum
Nature hike
Night games
No Bears Are Out Tonight (game)
Nursing home program
Opera
Paddle ball
Paint a house
Password
Picking wildflowers
Picnic (in a tree, in the rain, on the roof)
Pinball party
Pizza party
Planetarium
Plant a garden

Play pool
Pogo sticks
Popcorn balls
Pop popcorn
Powderpuff football
Progressive dinner
Prospecting
Puppet show
Quilting
Rabbit hunting
Races
Raking leaves
Rapelling
Reunions (family, school, friends)
Riding a tram
Riding cows
Roasting marshmallows
Rock hunting
Rodeo
Roller skating
Rolling downhill
Running through sprinklers
Sand castles
Sand fighting
Sand jumping
Scaling cliffs
Scavenger hunt
Scrapbooks
Scripture chase
Scuba diving
Shooting (rifles or bows)
Shopping

Sightseeing
Singing and playing guitar
Skateboarding
Skindiving
Skipping rocks
Sliding down gutters
Snorkeling
Soccer
Soccer on ice
Softball
Spaghetti dinner
Square dancing
Squirt gun fight
Stake dance
Staring contest
State capitol tour
Statue (game)
Steak fry
Street dance
Studying together
Sunrise hike
Sunbathing
Surfing
Surprise party
Swimming
Swinging
Swinging across canals
Swinging on ropes in a barn
Table tennis
Taffy pull
Talk-a-thon
Tape-recording your voices

Tennis
Tetherball
Tire changing
Toilet papering
Touring a fire station
Touring Church history sites
Track meet
Train ride
Trampoline
Trap shooting
Treasure hunt
Tunnel in a haystack
Turtle racing
TV
Twelve days of Christmas
Twister (game)
Ultimate Frisbee
Unicycle riding
Visiting a cemetery
Visiting a fish hatchery
Visiting a hospital
Visiting a monastery
Visiting a rest home
Visiting a shut-in
Visiting a travel agency
Visiting battlegrounds
Visiting Temple Square
Vocabulary game
Volleyball
Wading in a river
Walking
Walking a dog

Walking in the rain or snow
Washing a dog
Washing cars
Watching a sunrise or sunset
Watching fireworks
Watching planes take off and land
Water balloon fight
Water basketball
Watermelon bust
Water park
Water skiing
Water tubing (floating in inner tubes)
Weird table settings
Wheelbarrow racing
Window shopping
Winks Game
Wrestling
Zoo

Although some fun dates are spontaneous, most take planning and preparation. Use your imagination to come up with many more original, fun activities. Be creative, and you will create memories.

INDEX

Discipline, 145–51
Doctrine, false, 17–18, 24–25. *See also*
   Intellectuals, self-proclaimed;
   Satan
Dress, appropriate, 39–44, 57, 74–75,
   86

Education: continuing, 83–84;
   concentrating on, 87–88; seeking
   truth in, 90–95; while engaged,
   111; budgeting for, 154–55
Elitism, spiritual, 14–20
Enduring to the end, 174–78
Engagements, 105, 107–12
Examination, physical, 129
Example, 9–10, 76

Family, 9–13, 160
Fault finding, 30–31
Finances, 139–41, 152–56
For the Strength of Youth, 68
Fornication, 108
Friends, 4–5, 60–63, 74

Game, open-ended statement,
   100–101
Garments, temple, 41, 75
Goals, setting, 35, 78
Gratitude, 75–76
Growth, spiritual: during mission,
   1–2, 70; after mission, 5–8; to
   happen naturally, 45–49

Habits, irritating, 134
Hair length, 39, 43
Holidays, 165
Holy Ghost. *See* Spirit
Homesickness, 55
Homosexuality, 91–92
Honeymoon, yearly, 164
Humor, 12

Immodesty, 41–42
Inactivity, 22–23, 35–36, 157–59
Information gathering, 112
Integrity, 171–72

Intellectuals: self-proclaimed, 29–31,
   90–92; true spiritual, 32
Interview: personal worthiness, 37;
   job, 86
Intimacy: in dating, 67–68; in
   marriage, 125–30
Inventories, companionship, 131,
   133–37

Job hunting, 85–89
Job satisfaction, importance of, 81–82
Journal, missionary, 49

Kirtland Temple, example of not
   building, 118, 147–50
Kissing, 67–68
Knowledge, gospel, 16, 25–26, 94

Last days, the, 175–77
Leaders, criticizing, 31
Leadership, 64
Letter, writing to oneself, 36–37
Love, expressing, 156

Manners, 73
Mantle, of missionary work, 53–54
Marriage: window for, 68–69; to
   person who waited, 70; to person
   you date, 98; planning date of,
   110; planning temple, 111;
   problem solving in, 114–23,
   152–56; intimacy in, 124–30;
   resolving conflicts in, 131–37;
   decision making in, 138–44;
   changing patterns of behavior in,
   145–51; priesthood blessings in,
   157–60; developing good
   relationship in, 161–67; entering
   into covenant of, 174–78
Maturity, social, 63–64
McKay, David O. and Emma Rae,
   131–32
Mission, discussing, 37–38, 48
Mission, stake, 5–6
Mission field, returning to, 53–59
Mission president, visits with, 58, 73

190